PART ONE: AN INTRODUCTION

How I Became A Writer About Indigo People

Somehow, without expecting it, I've become something of an expert on indigo people.

Let me explain how this happened. When I was about eighteen I met my friend Christian, who identifies as indigo and who, after getting to know me for a while, decided that I must be indigo too.

My initial reaction was negative. I didn't like to think myself better than others (as his description of indigo seemed to suggest) and I suppose I didn't really like labels in general.

That said, over time Christian got through to me. I eventually realised that the indigo identification explained a whole lot about me, and gradually found myself becoming more comfortable in my own skin as my unusual traits started to seem more like positive things rather than strange and inexplicable flaws.

I began to look for other indigos. I'd place online classified ads, under the "friends" section, with a list of traits. I stuck up posters on the street for indigo workshops I was organising. I went to indigo meetups, such as I could find. I even had my then-girlfriend make a t-shirt with the word "INDIGO" on it in big capital letters, hoping it would start conversations.

Through this and my online life I came to know other indigos very well. I started to see patterns in their personalities and the problems which challenged them. When I wrote my article, "How To Tell If You Are Indigo" (www.sophiagubb.com/how-to-tell-if-you-are-indigo), I based it off my real life experience rather than rehashing what other people had written. Perhaps because of this originality, that article became very successful on Google and is to this day one of the biggest sources of traffic for my website, sophiagubb.com.

An interesting pattern I've seen in indigos is that once they've read my article, they tend to want to write me their entire life stories either in the comments or via a personal email. I've come to believe that indigos have an incredible need to be heard and understood, something which only another indigo can satisfactorily give them.

Seeing as I couldn't reply to all of these emails without making it a full time job, I started offering counselling on my website. Not intuitive counselling – more like just conversation having, or listener being. Over a couple of years I did quite a few counselling sessions, which taught me even more about the indigo personality.

So, this is why I feel qualified to write this book. I'm not a channeller, and I don't have a PhD in anything, but I do have a lot of experience with indigos, and importantly, I have a lot to say about them.

In fact, as this book is primarily targeted towards other indigos, to be exact I should say that I have a lot to say to *you*.

Terms

I think I have to start this book off with a discussion about terms.

"Indigo", or rather "indigo children" is a term that came from the author Nancy Ann Tappe. Nancy Ann Tappe was a person who experienced synesthesia, and literally perceived people as having or being represented by different colours. At one point, Nancy realised that a lot of new children being born were of an indigo hue. She mentioned them in her book, "Understanding Your Life Thru Colour".

Later, Lee Carroll and Jan Tober compiled a book called "Indigo Children: The New Kids Have Arrived". I believe this book was what popularised the indigo children concept.

Now, in this book, there was a channeling from an entity named Kryon. This contained the list of traits which so many people felt identified with:

They come into the world with a feeling of royalty (and often act like it)
They have a feeling of "deserving to be here," and are surprised when others don't share that.
Self-worth is not a big issue. They often tell the parents "who they are."
They have difficulty with absolute authority (authority without explanation or choice).

They simply will not do certain things; for example, waiting in line is difficult for them.
They get frustrated with systems that are ritually oriented and don't require creative thought.
They often see better ways of doing things, both at home and in school, which makes them seem like "system busters" (nonconforming to any system).
They seem antisocial unless they are with their own kind. If there are no others of like consciousness around them, they often turn inward, feeling like no other human understands them. School is often extremely difficult for them socially.
They will not respond to "guilt" discipline ("Wait till your father gets home and finds out what you did").
They are not shy in letting you know what they need.

(Excerpted from the indigochild.com website).

I believe these few lines started a movement, created a community (at least online) where many people finally felt like they could be understood and could understand themselves.

Now the main problem is that these people didn't really fit Nancy Ann Tappe's description of indigos. Particularly, Nancy said that indigos had suddenly started being born en masse at a certain date, and that all children born after a certain date were indigos. I've often said that if all kids nowadays were (Kryon) indigo, we'd be seeing non-violent demonstrations against imposed authority in all of our schools! Put that many system-busters together and what you have is a revolution. Oh, if only.

If you haven't already guessed, I will be talking about Kryon indigos in this book. Nancy Ann Tappe's version of indigos seems to be something entirely different to me, and irrelevant to what I want to talk about.

It's strange to be using the name she invented because of nothing but an apparent misunderstanding, I know. But it's hard to change now. Already, "indigo" is the accepted word for what Kryon described, and the only way I can reach those people is to use that word.

I will, however, be alternating the term "indigo" with the term "Wanderer" in this book. "Wanderer" is the word used in the Ra Channellings (The Law of One) to talk about what clearly seems to be the same thing as Kryon indigos. I'm hoping that by using "Wanderer" here, I can gently encourage others to transition into using this less misleading term.

What About Crystal Children?

I don't know what I think about the topic of crystal children or crystal people.

From the descriptions of crystal people I've read, they seem to be similar to indigo people but for perhaps two main differences:

1. They are even more sensitive than indigo people,

and 2. They tend to be more peaceful and accepting, not so much acting as warriors or rebels but instead more inclined to change the world through service, kindness, and positive energy. Indigos are disposed towards "shaking the world up", while crystals can be a bit more low key. I suspect, though, that crystals would be able to understand the impulses of the indigo.

I have also heard that Crystals take on externally similar auras to those around them, allowing them to function as chameleons and blend in with Earth society.

Because of this relatively small difference, I often ignore the concept of crystals, simply because it's difficult to filter the conflicting information I read about them -- and because I would act the same way whether or not crystals existed. I often bundle indigos and crystals together in my head, and use "indigo" as shorthand for "indigo or crystal".

According to two people who gave me their intuitive read of my energy, I might actually be a crystal myself, having transitioned from indigo to crystal in my early twenties*. This would make sense, as I no longer identify with the need to fight and rebel in the same way as I used to, and am more inclined to peaceful ways of helping the world. I no longer break unjust rules for no other reason than because they are unjust, seeing the benefit of avoiding unnecessary conflicts.

*According to Sunfell.com, these kind of transitions happen when someone has an "overlay" of a different soul colour which is then shed to reveal the true colour underneath. I have no way of verifying such an idea, so I take it with a pinch of salt.

That said, this isn't enough for me to feel certain about what I am. I simply don't know if the crystal concept is valuable for me, so I continue identifying as indigo when a label is necessary. More people recognise the term "indigo" anyway, and when I use the word it's in an attempt to connect with a certain understanding; so "indigo" works for me.

I think the term "Wanderer" sidesteps this confusion. As far as I can tell, it refers to both indigos and crystals, very much like my lazy way of using the term "indigo". Perhaps this is another reason why "Wanderer" may be a better term than "indigo" for our purposes.

I will still report on some of the things I've read about crystals later in the book, however, making my level of uncertainty in these concepts clear as I do so. It could be that other people find a benefit in the term which I haven't been able to so far personally.

Wanderer Traits, According To Me

So we have the Kryon indigo traits, including feeling like royalty, having a problem with imposed authority, tending to do things in your own way and "system busting".

Since that original list of traits, different channelers as well as indigos themselves have contributed to a more in-depth description of the Wanderer. I will now list and explain some of these additional traits, as well as explain a few of the Kryon traits a bit more in depth.

If you have already read my article "How To Tell If You Are Indigo", you might want to skip or skim this section.

- Wanderers tend to feel like they are not "from this world". The basic reason for this, at least if you believe in reincarnation, is that they are not. Most of their previous incarnations were in other worlds, worlds of higher vibration where things were simply better than here: people were kinder, things worked better, things made *sense*.

The effect of this is, even when they don't have conscious past life memories, an indigo tends to feel very estranged from this world. They see how things could be so much better and tend to just feel bewildered at how the people from this world act in such petty and cruel ways.

Some indigos go so far as to consider themselves alien, or in less extreme cases they show other signs of estrangement including being convinced that they were adopted, or born in the wrong place or at the wrong time. Indigos are the "black sheep" of their families or societies. Some travel a lot and move house often, going between countries or towns, subconsciously or consciously looking for the place they will feel at home. This search is rarely wholly satisfactory, because ultimately they are searching for something that doesn't exist on Earth. The closest they can find to that is to surround themselves with a "chosen family" of people who feel more like true family, and who help them feel that not everything is completely out of place here.

Occasionally, with other indigo friends I've gone so far as to refer to non-indigos as "humans" (implying that I am not a human). Other people sometimes invent other, varyingly disparaging terms for non-indigos, such as muggles, Others, Earth people, sheep, and so on. These days I prefer to avoid such terms because I don't like the sense of separation this creates. However, the Wanderer sense of alienation is evident in this tendency.

- As the Kryon traits explain, indigos have a problem with imposed authority and with systems that don't seem to make sense. They require reasonable explanations for a rule or an order, and when none are forthcoming, they can tell a hierarchy is being imposed. This should not be considered a quirk or a disorder, but rather a sign of a kind of instinctual intelligence plus enough internal dignity and willpower that they find it very hard to ignore what they feel.

Indigos are basically fundamentally anti-hierarchy. This comes in the form of an instinct. Even if you manage to brainwash an indigo into thinking that hierarchy is good, the instinct still makes it almost impossible to accept hierarchy. In the few moments in my life where I tried believing in hierarchy because I couldn't find any other solutions to my pit of despair, my instinct caused me in response to become pretty much disabled by depression; it simply wouldn't allow me to live in a certain way.

School is a hierarchical system with imposed authorities. As such, indigos almost invariably have difficulties in school. Some are more obviously rebellious than others, questioning teachers and leading protests against things they think are unjust. Others are quieter, but will inevitably suffer under hierarchy even if they don't tell anyone.

- Indigos need things to be authentic. They have a problem putting on a social mask. When required to by society, they often just isolate themselves instead. If they do try, it feels very unnatural and awkward.

Because of this inability to wear a mask, others might perceive indigos as especially authentic and individual. Or perhaps they will use less kind words.

Wanderers tend to have a strong bullshit detector, and can tell when someone is being inauthentic. They often have an extreme dislike for such people.

Because of their need to be authentic, indigos often have rather a disdain for small talk. They are not interested in feigning interest in things that they don't feel to matter. They prefer to have deep, authentic connections, and if these are hard to find the indigo might prefer one-on-one interactions where the other is likely to feel less bound by social conformity and can open up about things that actually matter.

School is usually hard for Wanderers, as the social environment there mandates putting on a social mask. Wanderers are usually unable to do this for long, and therefore tend to stand out and become a target for bullying.

- Indigos are highly sensitive. There is a term for this in fact: HSP (Highly Sensitive Person). I like to say that not all HSP are indigos, but all indigos are HSP.

Indigos tend to feel things on a much more intense level than non-indigos, sometimes excessively much so. This seems to be strongest in childhood, becoming more manageable later on, especially as the Wanderer learns to deal with it better.

Indigos are usually very empathic, meaning they often feel the feelings of other people as if they were their own. This often causes discomfort in public spaces or noisy environments, as the negative emotions and energies of a hundred people seem to be coming down on that person at once. Many times, indigos just can't go to loud parties, or if they do go they kind of have to force themselves because they don't really enjoy it.

Sometimes a Wanderer's sensitivity is too much, and this can in some cases lead the emotional system to shut down entirely, causing the indigo to seem like the exact opposite to sensitive: a robot. Don't be fooled, though; it's a defence mechanism.

- Indigos are "old souls". That is, they have reincarnated many times before this one. This can sometimes be evident when an indigo acts or feels old or seems to have a wisdom beyond their years.

I believe occasionally indigos might not be old souls in the strict sense because some of them have been angels or other high-vibration spirits who have done most of their evolution in the ether, and who are therefore fairly new to incarnating. However, these will probably still seem like "old souls" in terms of wisdom.

- Wanderers have a fast internal rhythm, which means that for them, the world seems to go way too slow and they want things to happen *faster*, always *faster*. This comes from the fact that in the high vibration worlds where indigos come from, reality responds to intention much faster and more effectively.

Because of this, I think many of us also really feel like we should be able to move objects with our mind, fly, manifest instantly, and so on. When it becomes clear in our childhood that we can't despite our best attempts, we feel frustrated.

Incidentally, this aspect of our origins is the reason behind Kryon's mention of waiting in line being hard for indigos. This trait is often diagnosed as ADHD, though it is up to every individual to decide whether they actually consider it a disorder or not. When understood and harnessed, I believe this can be a source of power.

- Indigos are highly creative and intelligent, often being considered "gifted kids". They tend to have multiple interests and, in line with their ADHD tendencies, often find it hard to focus on a single thing for a long time.

- Wanders are intense. Their internal energy is very strong, allowing for very strong emotions, strong determination, and vibrant self expression. They have a very strong will. When they use intention-manifestation or do other energy-based work, they are often quite powerful.

Many indigos report experiencing short-outs in electronics, flickering streetlamps, and light bulbs burning out when their emotions are intense and discordant.

- Wanderers often have an "addictive personality". They can fall prey to physical addictions such as drugs or food, or other addictions such as internet, television, or even unbalanced use of spirituality. It's important for an indigo to learn to deal with their sensitivity rather than numb themselves.

- Indigos are very idealistic and see how things should be different in the world. When they believe something, they usually believe in it strongly. They usually try to live consistently with their beliefs.

- Indigos feel a strong draw towards spirituality, personal development, and finding meaning. Even when they don't believe in spiritual stuff per se they tend to be very philosophical and might end up doing much the same things a "spiritual" person would do.

- Partly because of their sensitivity, partly because of their interest in spirituality, and partly because of their frustration with Earth's slow rhythm, indigos tend to have a difficulty with physicality and might be very "ungrounded". This means they might be prone to daydreaming, clumsy, floaty and impractical. They might feel disconnected from their body or find it very easy to "pop out" from their body to go explore other realms. They also might be prone to escapism, e.g. through books or video games. It's imperative for most indigos to work on this, because only when we are connected to this reality can we have a chance to influence it.

- Indigos feel a sense of purpose, a need to change the world for the better. They usually don't initially know what they are supposed to do, just that there is something they have to do. This can lead to a lot of frustration until the indigo finally finds their purpose. ← * yes*

- Indigos tend to have a stronger natural talent for psychic abilities than most, though as with anyone the talent could be latent or suppressed, so it doesn't really mean anything if an indigo doesn't show signs of psychic abilities. They might manifest as what seems like nothing but a good intuition, which in fact is all psychic abilities are anyway.

- In my own experience, indigos have very steady gazes. They might learn to avoid looking into someone's eyes for too long so that that person doesn't get uncomfortable, but if you challenge them to a staring contest, they will be a worthy opponent. Uninhibited, a Wanderer's gaze seems to pierce through layers of pretense to see the very soul inside.

- I'd like to add something about the "feeling of royalty" mentioned in the Kryon channeling. I think this one doesn't always fit. Indigos may be arrogant but are not always so, and due to their aversion towards hierarchy would be unlikely to feel comfortable if they happened to be literal royalty or anything approaching that (though they might seek positions of power if they feel that it's the only alternative to being someone's subordinate).

Instead, think of it as referring to a a strong sense of internal dignity, an awareness that being placed on a lower rung to someone else is unbecoming of you. Even though indigos sometimes do come to have low self-esteems due to the circumstances of their lives, they usually still have a kind of instinct which makes it hard for them to accept a lower-caste existence.

- Wanderers often experience depression because of their sensitivity, difficulty with the world they live in, and isolation.

- They may also experience chronic anger because of their internal sense of dignity conflicting with the standard anti-self-esteem processing of Earth society.

- Wanderers also unusually often have big life challenges they have to go through, particularly in childhood, such as a major disease, accident, disability, surviving abuse, being a minority, moving to a new country, being transgender, and so on. There doesn't seem to be much commonality to where these difficulties come from, just that there is some kind of major difficulty.

A Wanderer's body is quite sensitive to toxins, though, which may explain some of the diseases. It's often important for an indigo to experiment and find a diet that works for them.

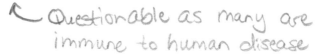
Questionable as many are immune to human disease

- Some indigos find themselves hounded all their lives by paranormal events, such as seeing ghosts, predictive dreams, reading thoughts, UFO sightings, and so on. I put this last because despite being one of the things that is most focused on when talking about indigos, I think it's one of the least essential traits.

Note that while Wanderers are described as being "old souls", are of "high vibration" and their previous incarnations come from a "high vibration" world or dimension, there is a difference between their soul and their incarnation. When someone is incarnated they do not automatically express every aspect of their soul. A person's personality changes over a lifetime, while their soul, which has developed over thousands of years, changes relatively little. As we, within a single incarnation, evolve towards a greater understanding of ourselves, we become more and more like the soul we have inside, accessing the things we have learned in lives before, getting more in touch with our talents, and being more "true to ourselves". On the other hand, traumas or other unfavorable situations can cause us to build up a layer of extraneous "stuff" that covers up our soul and leads us further and further away from our true selves.

All this leads up to the fact that, while indigos are "high vibration" inside - that is, they are kind, peaceful, wise, and generally beautiful people - the outside personality doesn't always show that. Sometimes a Wanderer gets lost by trying to fit in (despite the screaming of their soul) or gets hurt so badly they get into destructive cycles, unleashing their pain on others or themselves. They might not always be "good people" or "spiritual people". Because of their sensitivity and intensity, when indigos go bad they can sometimes go *really* bad. Some suggest that some school shootings were caused by indigos bullied by their peers. I can't confirm that, yet, I have heard of or met indigos who were very self-destructive or went so far as to hurt others. In my time, I've also done a bit of both.

I've noticed, however, that despite being consumed by hatred at certain times in my life, I mostly held back from my most violent urges. I believe even then, the calling of my soul was tempering my actions.

I think even when a Wanderer is in a very dark time, it's possible for perceptive people - especially other Wanderers - to see through that darkness and see the kindness and idealism under their torment.

So How Do You Know If You Are Indigo?

A lot of people come out of the list of traits with a lot of doubts still about whether they are Wanderers. I've given counselling sessions to a few, and the truth is I haven't really found a satisfactory answer for these people.

I think the most unambiguous Wanderer trait is if you have a strong feeling of having come from another planet, one where things are better. Not all indigos have such an unambiguous feeling, but if you do have it, that would make things pretty clear.

You might also want to meditate on this. Earnestly ask yourself, *Where do I come from?* If the answer doesn't come immediately, then just leave that question there and go through the next few days or weeks with a feeling of expectancy. Your subconscious mind will work on it, and answers will pop up as you go about your daily life.

If you don't have an explicit feeling telling you that you came from another planet, at least I think it's essential that you feel on some level that you are *not from here.*

Another good thing to look at is whether you are a *system-buster* or have an *instinctual rejection of imposed authority.* At the very least, you can exclude yourself from being indigo if you find it easy to follow authority and don't mind not knowing *why* you are being told to do something.

Once, with my friend Christian I developed a half-joking "indigo test". It involved engaging in some very extroverted and clownish humour: for example, imitating a crazy turkey. Non-indigo people often looked at us like we were crazy, and tried to distance themselves from us. Indigo people, having less attachment to social ideas of decorum and properness, tended to laugh. (This works especially well in more uptight cultures).

Another good thing to note if you are unsure is the difference between bolder/more extroverted Wanderers and the quieter ones. The bolder ones are more likely to be recognised as indigo, as their anti-system and anti-authoritarian tendencies are more obvious. The quieter ones may prefer to avoid standing out, but will still resist authority in subtle ways, and will absolutely suffer in hierarchies and systems, even if they don't show it.

It's Down To You

Ultimately, however, I think the problem is that there is nothing that can definitively prove that someone is an indigo. All of these traits *can* be found in non-indigos. Some think that this makes the concept useless; I think it just means you have to depend on your internal feelings, rather than expecting anything external to bring you a definitive answer.

What do you feel when you read the indigo traits? Does it make you light up, and feel, *"someone finally understands me!"*? Does it make something inside you stir? Do you have a strange intuition that what you are reading is important?

The ultimate test for whether you want to identify as indigo is whether it helps you in some way. Perhaps the self understanding lets you finally accept yourself as you are, or it lets you feel like you're not so strange and different after all. Perhaps it lets you find other people like you, people who can finally truly understand you.

If you get these good results from identifying as indigo, who cares if it's real or not? And if you don't get any good results from identifying as indigo, what is the point?

What About The Forer Effect?

The Forer Effect is something that is often brought up by skeptics of the Wanderer concept. According to Wikipedia:

> *In 1948, psychologist Bertram R. Forer gave a psychology test ... to a group of his psychology students who were told that they would each receive a brief personality vignette or sketch based on their test results. ... Forer gave each student a purportedly individualized sketch and asked each of them to rate it on how well it applied. In reality, each student received the same sketch, consisting of the following items:*

1. *You have a great need for other people to like and admire you.*
2. *You have a tendency to be critical of yourself.*
3. *You have a great deal of unused capacity which you have not turned to your advantage.*
4. *While you have some personality weaknesses, you are generally able to compensate for them.*
5. *Your sexual adjustment has presented problems for you.*
6. *Disciplined and self-controlled outside, you tend to be worrisome and insecure inside.*
7. *At times you have serious doubts as to whether you have made the right decision or done the right thing.*
8. *You prefer a certain amount of change and variety and become dissatisfied when hemmed in by restrictions and limitations.*
9. *You pride yourself as an independent thinker and do not accept others' statements without satisfactory proof.*

   ...

On average, the students rated its accuracy as 4.26 on a scale of 0 (very poor) to 5 (excellent). Only after the ratings were turned in was it revealed that each student had received an identical sketch assembled by Forer from a newsstand astrology book. ...

In a later study mentioned in the same Wikipedia article, test subjects were more likely to accept the vague generalities as correct than a *genuine personality evaluation*.

So, perhaps the Wanderer concept is so vague and feel-good that anyone can identify with it?

I have my own concerns in this area. I think the concept is vague enough in some ways that non-indigos might come to identify with the term, or perhaps succumb to *wanting* to identify with it. In places where I've met indigos, both online and offline, I've found both what I consider genuine indigos and people who seemed to me to have rather big egos and just wanted to be seen as different or special.

In my experience, though, it's quite easy to tell them apart. It's not like real Wanderers never have big egos, but those who fool themselves that they are Wanderers are having their actions entirely *dictated* by their egos, which I think indigos rarely do to that extent. The ones who are fooling themselves are prone to airy-fairy spiritual bullshit but show little actual insight and rarely *do* anything to make good on their words. When you talk with them (supposing you are a Wanderer), you won't feel that same resonance you feel when you talk with a real Wanderer.

As for the accusation of the indigo traits being excessively vague? Honestly, I think they are not, and that certain dogmatic skeptics bring up the Forer effect because they are doing what dogmatic skeptics do, that is, try and discredit anything that isn't written in a mainstream University textbook.

Not so many people out there are unbearably uncomfortable with imposed authority. This is proven by the popularity of white-collar jobs. If everyone reacted to imposed authority the same way indigos do, then society as we know it would look VERY different.

Not everyone is so sensitive they find it hard to be in large crowds or noisy parties. Not everyone experiences a very strong drive to do something to change the world for the better. The list goes on.

Really, I don't see what is so vague about this. Sure, I guess most people can find in their hearts SOME discomfort with imposed authority and large crowds and a desire to change the world for the better. But few people find those traits genuinely force their lives down a different path. Most people bow down to authority and give up on making a change. Indigos may find themselves compromising on their instinctual values, but the need to actualise who they are never goes away, and the calling even gets stronger over time, making them *literally sick* unless they heed it. They just can't be "well adjusted" in the modern world.

Compare this to

You have a great need for other people to like and admire you. You have a tendency to be critical of yourself. You have a great deal of unused capacity which you have not turned to your advantage.

I think it's obvious that we are talking about different things here.

If this still doesn't convince you, try reading through the comments on my indigo article. There have been people reduced to tears by what they read, who found their way out of depression because of it, even one or two who think the information might have saved their life. Whatever that is, that's not airy-fairy. It's hitting a chord.

The Use Of The Label

These days I rarely think about being a Wanderer. I sort of had my indigo phase, and I left that behind after a while, except for giving counselling and writing this book.

I think my indigo phase was very important. It helped develop my self understanding, helped get me out of my shell, and helped me develop new ways of interacting with the world. It stopped me feeling like a freak or like I was crazy, and gave me a new appreciation for aspects of myself that were different or odd. It gave me a much needed feeling of validation.

I also think that leaving my indigo phase behind was important for me. The main reason is, I do find that identifying as indigo tends to make me feel separated from others. It's usually understood that indigo people are somehow *more evolved* than other people, and while I do believe that I have gifts in compassion, insight and wisdom, I very much dislike the feeling I get when I focus on that and compare myself to others. My ego gets tangled up in it, and it's too easy to get a superiority complex. And even if I manage to keep my ego out of it, it tends to hurt the egoes of others when I mention it.

I think this is the reason I initially resisted accepting the term, in fact. Actually, at least 50% of the people I think are indigo initially resist the term, often never coming to accept it. I tease them that since they don't want to be called indigo, I am now *even more* sure that they are indigo.

I don't think fear of your own ego is a good reason to avoid identifying as indigo. If nothing else, learning to accept your own power and spiritual attunement is a good exercise in mastering your ego. Arrogance and false modesty are two sides of the same coin: ultimately the only healthy way of seeing yourself is *accurately*, including an accurate assessment of your strengths.

I suggest using the indigo term for as long as it's useful, and then leaving it behind. Hold it at arm's length, if you must. Use it to learn about yourself and to find others who understand you. This book will hopefully give you some tools to do just that.

Additionally, I suggest being careful about trying to place other people into the box of indigo or non-indigo. While this can be helpful initially to help you find others who are like you, it can also hurt people's feelings; non-indigo friends might feel inadequate, and others might feel you are giving them a label without their consent. Classify people as needed, but be sensitive about it. And when you are ready, give up this practice. The world doesn't need to be split into two separate factions. That happens enough already.

Kristen

I learnt a lot about Wanderers from an indigo called Kristen Finlayson, both from reading her blog and from personal correspondence with her. We all have "guide" figures who appear in our lives, sometimes for a short time and sometimes for a long time, and Kristen was one of those to me.

I've tried to make sure that this book contains all the information which I gained from her, though sometimes I've felt it best to simply paste in quotes from her, as she expressed things better than I ever could. I feel justified in doing so because her website went down (and I lost contact with her) and otherwise this information would simply disappear. I've also compiled a page of her writing, with the intention of preserving it, that can be found on my website at sophiagubb.com/k.

PART TWO: YOUR BASIC NEEDS

In this section I will go over some of the basic needs which indigos have, especially at the early stages of coming to terms with who they are. In each case I'll explain how you might be able to deal with each need.

One of the biggest needs which Wanderers have is recognition. Everyone needs recognition, but Wanderers are so different from most people that they can often feel especially alone.

While non-Wanderers can fulfill your social needs to some extent, I believe there is a part of a Wanderer that can only be fully understood by another Wanderer. If you have never met someone like yourself, it's likely that you've had a chronic feeling of being constantly a bit lonely even when amongst people. You might have yearned for someone who could truly see who you are inside.

The simple answer is to look for other indigos. How? Well, there are a few ways...

The more obvious way for meeting other indigos is to just get to the point. Look for indigo meetups or gatherings (they are rare, but you might be lucky enough to find one). Write classified ads including a list of indigo traits. Go onto indigo forums online.

Not everyone who calls themselves indigo is a true indigo. Beware that at least some of these people will be nutjobs. If you can filter through those, though, you should be able to find a lot of true indigos this way.

Finding Other Indigos

Apart from this obvious method, I'd like to suggest a rather universal rule: *if you want to find someone like you, go to the places where you would go if you were like you.*

Does this sound flippant? I think it is anything but. The thing is, a lot of the time we aren't going to the places we would go if we were like us. We try to fit in and go to "normal" things. We put up with boring "normal" friends because we don't think we can do better. We don't have the bravery to push our boundaries and check out new places. Or maybe we're just not getting out of the house at all.

I like to say, do something you'd like to do, something you're interested in, and just make a little extra effort to be a bit more social about it. If you like to write, you could write at home or you could go to a writer's meetup to exchange ideas. If you like yoga, you could do it at home or go to classes. And so on.

The particular things which Wanderers are drawn to most are those involving spirituality, personal development, creativity and bucking the system. You might find them in an anarchist meetup, involved in Unschooling, doing meditation, in vegan meetups, in any sort of activism, in "rebellious" pursuits, and so on. I believe if you just make enough effort to go out and explore new scenes, you will find people like you.

The worst place to meet indigos is in school or in a "normal" job. There is almost no filter for the people in these environments at all, and indigos are about 1 person in 100, so you do the math. If you're stuck in an environment like this, be sure to spend your free time in places where more specific types of people are likely to congregate.

If You Can't Find Other Indigos In Real Life

The best thing is to find fellow Wanderers in real life. If you can't manage that, or if you're still working on that and need something to bear you through until you get there, there are two options:

1. Find a friend who can *mostly* get you.

If you can't find an indigo, then someone who is a little introverted, a little deep, and a little questioning will do. You need someone you can talk to about the things that are on your mind and who will understand and acknowledge you. Older people are often better than younger people, as they tend to be less shallow. People who are in some way minorities or outcasts are often better than "normal" people, as they will be less judgmental. Or else you can simply look for someone who shares one of your more alternative interests.

Besides this, people tend to be deeper and less conformist when alone than when in groups. Try getting some one-on-one time with someone who seems promising.

2. Find indigo friends online.

It's much more fulfilling to have friends in real life than online, but if you can't find Wanderers in real life, the internet does have the benefit that different sorts of people are a lot easier to find.

Forums such as IndigoSociety.com and the Indigo Adults Moderated Yahoo group are good places to meet other Wanderers. Go and interact a bit, and perhaps you'll find someone who is willing to have long conversations online - be it through written text or perhaps Skype - who will be able to fulfill some of your need to be recognised for who you are.

Note that as someone who has possibly been a loner all their life, it can be easy to rationalise away your feelings and say that you don't need people anyway. You do - everyone does. If you doubt it, consider, as an extreme example, that solitary confinement in prisons is considered a form of torture by many psychologists. It can cause madness and hallucinations.

You may be better than most at dealing with excessive solitude, but that doesn't mean that it is actually good for you. Perhaps you have never felt what it's like to feel completely fulfilled as far as your social needs are concerned, and you somehow assume that this constant feeling of hollowness is just how life is supposed to be.

Facing up to the fact that you have dealt with heart-rending alienation all your life can hurt, which is why it can feel better in the short term to pretend you don't have these needs. Western society might support you in that, with its message of hard individualism. In Western society, it's often seen as "cool" not to depend on anyone.

But we do. We're human. Accept that. Go out and find someone who will understand you.

About Anti-Authoritarianism

As a Wanderer, anti-authoritarianism and anti-hierarchy is in your blood. Even if you *try* to accept imposed authorities, you will find that you just can't. Submitting to hierarchy feels like death to an indigo.

When someone orders you to do something, you ask "Why?". If their answer is unsatisfactory, your instinct is to defy the order. It's possible you've been abused to the point where you have to suppress yourself and just follow the orders, but this feels unbelievably uncomfortable.

Authority or official qualifications don't mean anything in particular to you. Neither does tradition. You have an instinct that these things have been constructed as ways of controlling people, getting them to follow without question. You, however, still question them.

You prefer things that are meaningful, whose reason to exist can be clearly explained without "because I say so" or "that's just how it is". School history lessons seem like endless bullshit - if you learn history, you want to know about people's lives and the deeper meaning of events. Petty bureaucracy or other meaningless structures drive you to a rage.

It's likely that you will be labelled as "defiant", "having issues with authority", or otherwise pathologised. I'm here now to say: what you have is not a pathology. It is an instinct to truth. You *know* deep down that imposed authority is wrong, just because it *is*. In this conviction you are *more* healthy than the others, not less. But when you live in a world of sick people, being healthy might look strange and undesirable.

Especially if you are still a child, you will likely come under a lot of pressure to conform to hierarchy. You may even be given special attention so as to "fix" you, such as being sent to a separate school for "difficult" children, or drugged. When going through this, just remember, *you* are right. It may seem like you against the world, but you are actually not alone; other indigos are out there. We know what you know: that this world is insane. You're not just imagining it.

Obedience is not a virtue.

School

School is a very hard time for most Wanderers. For those who are forced to go to school, I'm not sure what advice I can give. You cannot expect to thrive in this environment; the best you can hope for is damage control.

What I did in school was to try my best to choose where I placed my attention, keeping it for myself rather than giving it away, and using it on thinking about interesting things and trying to develop myself internally. Asides from that I often tried to disrupt the class with jokes, something that kept me feeling like I had some smidgen of control in this prison-like environment.

Later on, when I came to acknowledge my own feelings about school better, I began to skip classes and become more openly defiant. I eventually quit school. To be exact, I decided that I wouldn't back down when a teacher tried to tell me what to do, and that quickly turned into me having to leave.

I don't know if I can really recommend this strategy to anyone. What I suppose I was doing right in the end was recognising my own feelings about the system and not thinking I was crazy. Perhaps doubting myself would have been better to keep the situation stable, but I felt a lot healthier when I shed that pattern.

If I had to do it all again, I would have quit school earlier and/or asked my parents to move me to a free/democratic/anarchist school such as Summerhill in the UK. These schools are unique in that they don't issue orders to children; children are allowed to study or not study, as they choose. Perhaps a Wanderer like you will find this unsurprising, but they usually choose to study, simply because, well, who wouldn't want to learn useful and interesting things if they weren't being forced to?

Children who enter a free school later on in their school career often go through a phase of acting out against the control they previously experienced. They tend to spend all their time doing non-school activities, all those things their previous teachers would not have allowed them to do. Eventually, they start to feel able to participate in classes again, no longer feeling like it's something disempowering for them.

Something to be aware of is that this period of adaptation takes longer the longer a child has been in a "normal" school. Some free schools won't accept children after a certain age because they tend to find it too hard to get used to the freedom. Hopefully, though, you should be able to get through this transition cleanly, having your indomitable Wanderer instincts to guide you.

If you're lucky, you might also have parents who might consider homeschooling using the Radical Unschooling philosophy. Radical Unschooling is the home counterpart to free schools: it means not ordering a child about or trying to control them. Few parents are able or willing to get involved in this sort of parenting, but perhaps if you direct them to some resources (the book Radical Unschooling by Dayna Martin for example) there might be a chance.

Jobs

Very opinionated writing style. Debatable things and statements within book. Still good intro to everything

In general, life after school is so, so much better than life before school. The simple fact of being able to make your own major life decisions, and to get away from would-be dictators (teachers and parents), is unbelievably freeing.

However, you're probably aware that many jobs are very hierarchical. At worst, this can be "out of the frying pan into the fire", as they say. However, the wonderful thing about jobs is that you're not legally obliged to do them, and you have a certain amount of power over which jobs you take.

I believe that most white-collar jobs are hierarchical and thus, a very bad choice for an indigo. If you try and squeeze yourself into such an ill-fitting environment, you'll pay for it with your mental health. It takes some creativity, therefore, to work out something that will work for you.

I originally thought that the answer was to reject jobs entirely, and go for either freelance work or running my own business. I even had an unpleasant stint as a homeless person, which I considered better than the imagined alternative of a hierarchical work environment. I've chilled out a lot since then, and have recently finally gotten my first "real job" as a caterer for a small IT company. The environment in this company is not overly hierarchical, and I feel comfortable there - certainly a lot more comfortable than when I was dealing with horrible financial instability.

Since getting this job I've started to reconsider my original position on jobs in general. I still believe that freelance work or running one's own business are excellent options for Wanderers. However, I believe that jobs like mine - in small companies, with co-workers whose personalities support your wellbeing - can be quite okay. I even wonder if bigger companies or organisations might work for Wanderers on exceptional occasions. It's all about who you work with - if they are evil, then it'll be horrible, but if they are idealistic and kind, perhaps even Wanderers themselves, then you can have a good time.

I've long had the idea that getting higher qualifications might not be a good idea because qualifications in themselves are a proof of being able and willing to deal with hierarchy and Systems (school and university) and one can only expect that to lead to more hierarchy and Systems. Nowadays, as I've mellowed out, I've come to consider that even if this is true in general, there might be some strategies involving higher education that can still lead to acceptable outcomes.

What I can say is that it doesn't seem to make sense to get qualifications just because those around you pressure you to do so. Think about what you want to do, and then think about what you need to do to get there, and whether it would be worth the effort. I sense that being a psychotherapist would be a good path for me, for example, but the level of bullshit required to get an official qualification for that makes me consider other paths.

If you don't know what you want to do, then perhaps it's better to take a sabbatical until you're ready to commit to investing in qualifications. Getting a qualification just for the sake of it and then ending up doing something else would seem like a horrible waste of money and energy. That goes for anyone, but it could be especially taxing for a Wanderer.

My Own Career Path

My own career path has looked a little like this:

Homeless person - cook in return for food and a place to sleep - attempted professional reiki practitioner - freelance English teacher (in Spain) - writing while supported by a romantic partner - attempting to live radically cheap so I could live off my small website income - trying to get German government benefits - cook.

I chose most of these occupations because I could make them work freelance, though few exceptions, none of them worked that well, and I ended up needing my parents' support to survive. I think it took a lot of internal work on grounding (see page ***) and self love to get past my blocks in this area, and now I'm finally in a situation which feels comfortable, both in terms of financial security and what I'm doing with my time.

Although I've never done them, I've also considered sex work and computer programming fairly seriously. The first can be an option for indigos, who aren't influenced by socially imposed "morality" in the same way as Earth people. Done freelance through online ads, it provides a lot of free time and autonomy. Computer programming has also been interesting to me as it has few or no requirements in terms of bullshit official qualifications, earns quite well in proportion to the time you invest in it, and it can be done freelance.

I understand money-earning as a delicate balance between different factors: on the one hand, living your purpose, earning money, having a good time and contributing to society, and on the other hand any investment towards skills and official qualifications that might be necessary. You want to maximise each of the positive things and minimise the negative things, and it can be a bit of a head-breaker to work out which path would be optimal for you.

Naturally, you want to earn money while living your purpose. Relegating your purpose to your so-called "free time" is a perfect recipe for feeling unfree in the rest of your time. You won't always succeed in earning money from your purpose, especially if you have an urgent need for money here and now and can't spend all your time working towards a future perfect career, but you can hope for your work to at least fulfill you partly in this regard. My cooking work, for example, fulfills some aspect of my purpose (vegan cooking being an expression of compassion towards animals) and also allows me an outlet for my creativity, which is psychologically very nourishing.

Ultimately, it took a lot of grounding work (see page ***) to help me learn to see these matters in a practical way and deal with them effectively. It really is a good idea to work on this, as money will be an aspect of your life forever, whether you like it or not, and if you're going to play the game you might as well play it well. The more I've become grounded, the more comfortable I've been dedicating large amounts of my energy to this matter. It may be annoying seeing as Indigo World doesn't have money, and you might feel indignant about having to "earn" your right to exist, but rebelling against it hurts only you.

On Money

Many Wanderers will suddenly be feeling acutely uncomfortable after reading that previous section. The reason is that money is a very difficult concept for an indigo to grasp. We subconsciously remember a world without money, where people just *gave* to each other, and we know it was better.

Money in this world, or rather, the threat of having no money, is one of the ways in which hierarchy is reinforced. We are forced to go to school and do things we don't like on the principle that otherwise we might end up on the street someday. We're forced to do stupid useless jobs that go against our ideals and drain our energy on that same principle.

In the indigo world - well there are many but for simplicity we can talk about it as if it were just a single one - in Indigo World no one would ever end up on the streets. We, as indigos, rightly see such a world as allows this to be barbaric.

We know that it's not because of any real lack that people end up on the streets. We know that this possibility exists as a means of threatening us so that we conform to the system. The natural response to this is resistance. For this reason I think a lot of Wanderers end up on the streets or close to it; they feel disempowered by having to play this game, and would rather just quit in the first place.

You can try quitting; there are people who live without money. I even tried it myself, for a time. It was interesting, but took up a huge amount of my energy. Ultimately, I don't think that doing this is worth it if it reduces your ability to perform your soul purpose in this world. Giving up money is for some a matter of principle, but there is a difference between actions borne of nothing but principle, and actions which create real change in the world. I believe it is the latter actions which will have a lasting impact.

Avoid the financial hierarchy by being on top of the whole thing.

Because of this, I feel that it's important for indigos to learn to play the money game. You don't have to become one of the people who victimise others through money, but you should at least manage not to be victimised yourself. This means covering all of your basic needs, and I should mention that being able to enjoy yourself and not be uncomfortable is a basic need.

It has helped me to consider that it is not money itself which creates the threat of destitution. Money is a means of exchange. This might not be necessary on a world where things truly function in terms of *"from those of the greatest ability to those of the greatest need"* -- but it can at least be *understandable* that when people don't expect to be unconditionally supported by their society, they might want to engage in trade. It's a fair solution for the problem our society presents, and I don't think there is anything inherently wrong with it.

If money was simply given unconditionally to those who needed it things wouldn't be so bad. Ultimately, if we took this way of thinking far enough, we wouldn't need money at all. But in a world that is transitioning to that sort of economy, money makes temporary sense.

In political terms, I believe we should put a lot of energy behind campaigning for the Unconditional Basic Income. This is one step towards our Indigo World, made into an understandable concept. The idea is that everyone in our societies should receive a monthly income supplement, enough to cover basic needs, with no conditions, whatever their actual income is. In Canada this was done once on a small scale (google: Mincome) and no one turned into lazy slobs watching TV all day. But you knew that already, didn't you?

Unjobbing

I've already mentioned Unschooling, and the process which many conventionally schooled children go through to adapt to it, consisting of rebelliousness that continues until the child finally sort of realises that there's nothing to rebel against anymore. This process is called "deschooling".

I believe a similar process can happen as an adult. You can choose to transition to a non-hierarchical work environment, and/or simply work on removing your internalised authority figure.

An internalised authority figure is basically a voice in your head that replicates what your parents and teachers told you. It tells you, you *have* to do this or that. As the Wanderer you are, you naturally rebel. This can result in deadlock, where you need to do something but don't want to, and hold off on it for as long as reasonably possible. In practice, this means depression, procrastination, or escapism.

Dejobbing means learning to not replicate these voices. Put simply: stop bossing yourself about in your head. Stop "beating yourself up" to get yourself to do something. When you can manage that, then you should be able to find a much cleaner, more natural source of motivation.

In my blog, I've recommended engaging with this process by simply doing nothing. Just as children are set free until they realise they want to be responsible of their own accord, you can also be as irresponsible as possible until you're able to feel the need to be responsible without beating yourself up to make yourself do it.

In practice, that's what I've done, though I'm wondering if there isn't a better way of doing it. For someone who didn't have the financial support I had, that may not be possible at all.

I think the important thing is to come to identify the internalised voices of authority in your head, and to begin to choose other voices. When you're trying to motivate yourself to do something, be alert and try and see what sort of voice are you using. When you've identified your internal voice, you can make the choice to change it; talk to yourself the way you'd want to be talked to. Peacefully, in a friendly way. "Hey, can you do this for me? Thanks."

These thoughts are quieter and gentler than violent thoughts, so perhaps to start with they may seem less powerful. But as you remove the influence of your internalised authority figure, I believe they will become stronger.

Basically, the idea is to do everything because you "choose" to rather than because you feel you "should" do it.

Another thing that I've found helps is self love. Simply asking myself "What is the kindest thing I can do for myself right now?" helps me find a voice or motivation that is gentle and not violent. In fact, the pursuit of unjobbing tangentially led into my discovery of self love.

There's a whole book to write on this sometime. For now, try simply becoming aware of the your internal voices, and start making gentler choices, ones that reflect your own will rather than that of an internalised authority figure.

PART THREE: UNDERSTANDING AND RESPONDING TO YOUR INDIGO NATURE

As a Wanderer, you have a different nature to those around you. In this section, I'll help you understand that nature and suggest what to do about it.

Awakening And Forgetting

In the channelled work "The Law of One", Ra explains that Wanderers could be considered either brave or foolhardy, depending on your perspective, as they incarnate on this planet knowing the risk that they may forget their mission and become lost in this world's vibration. In the worst case, they may need further lifetimes on this planet to work through karma they've created here.

Ra states that (as of the channelling, in 1981) about 9% of Wanderers on Earth have a good idea of what they are and what their mission is. You are almost certainly one of them, seeing as you are reading this book. Additionally:

"There is a larger ... group [who understand] that they are not of this, shall we say, "insanity." This amounts to a bit over fifty percent of the remainder. Nearly one-third of the remainder are aware that something about them is different, so you see there are many gradations of awakening to the knowledge of being a Wanderer."

The term "indigo" or "Wanderer", or perhaps similar terms such as "starseed" or "lightworker", are all important to becoming "awakened" as an indigo. You need to be able to understand that you are indeed different somehow to be able to act on that knowledge. Some may also be able to "awaken" well enough simply by understanding that they are *not from here* and developing an understanding of their spiritual purpose in life.

Those who have a less clear understanding of what they are will accordingly be further away from their purpose in being here. These Wanderers are to differing degrees "lost" in the Earth's vibration, being less effective in creating change. You could say that they are soldiers that have fallen in this attempt to storm the fortress. OK, that sounds rather too martial for something that is really not of a martial nature, but perhaps some hint of meaning gets through.

The truly fallen are those who have no or little idea of what they are, and who have truly sunk into attempting to fit in in this world. These attempts never fully work, and the fallen Wanderer becomes plagued with depression, anxiety, sickness, suicidality, and other issues. Occasionally, some kind of equilibrium is found where the Wanderer can survive in a stable state in a "normal" life, but there is an immense amount of suffering underneath this seemingly successful exterior.

The worst case is when a Wanderer becomes consumed by addiction, madness, violence, or bitterness. They can be kind of "bipolar" personalities, showing moments of kindness and peace, and moments where they are consumed by darkness. Compared to other fallen souls, they stand out because they are not at all at home in their darkness. They still struggle to find a way out (compare to the average career criminal, who may find a certain stability within the chaos of their lifestyle). It's a state of absolute desperation.

So there are "awakened" indigos and "lost" indigos. Hopefully, this book will at least help you find the way to being awakened, if you're not already there.

As a side note, sunfell.com explains that some indigos, particularly those of previous generations, started out with an "overlay" of a different soul colour in order to protect themselves in society. This overlay would later be shed, revealing an indigo personality/energy underneath. So, someone might start out as almost a "normal" person before awakening to their indigo selves. A similar process would allow a crystal person to start life as an indigo and later become outwardly crystal in personality/energy. I have no idea how much truth is in these ideas.

On ADHD

Attention Deficit Hyperactivity Disorder (ADHD) is a diagnosis that is often given to Wanderers as children. Some say that all ADHD sufferers are actually indigos. I wouldn't go that far, but I would suspect that if I went to an ADHD self help group, I'd find some friends.

I was never diagnosed with ADHD, but then I grew up in the UK in the 90s, which is different from say, the USA in the 2010s. ADHD diagnosis has become more and more popular, as the psychiatry industry is seeing just how much money it can make from it.

As far as I can tell, it's enough to simply not be paying attention in class to be diagnosed as ADHD. Not paying attention in class doesn't mean you have a "deficit" of attention, it just means you don't feel like paying attention to this specific thing. Ultimately, ADHD diagnoses are mostly simply a tool for controlling children.

Mind you, Wanderers do have the fast internal rhythm I mentioned, and this can sometimes make things difficult if you don't understand how to deal with it. The solution is twofold: firstly you need to learn to understand and work with the rhythm itself, and secondly you need to become more grounded, which is a solution to a lot of the problems which Wanderers face. I will deal with both of these things in depth later on.

Another reason that indigos might stand out in this case is that they have a lot of internal energy. This can translate into nervousness if they are forced to sit still and do things which they can't -- (or don't want to -- use as outlets for their energy. You are probably more likely to feel in your element when learning enthusiastically about the things that interest you or being creative. Probably, the only real solution for this is to escape the "normal" school system and find a Free School or some parents willing to Unschool you.

If this is not possible, I hope I can at least infuse you with the self confidence to stand your ground if someone attempts to diagnose you or drug you. Just remember, you don't have to believe in their pseudoauthoritative bullshit. You are your own authority. You choose what happens to your body. Doctors and psychologists often want to make decisions for you, and when the whole world seems against you it can be hard to fight that, but ultimately YOU must consent to any medical stuff that happens to you. This is both your moral and your legal right.

I will add to all this, however, that some people do find their ADHD diagnosis empowering. For some people anti-ADHD drugs like Adderall seem to contribute to their quality of life. I'm not here to tell you what to think, only to remind you that there is more than one way of seeing things.

On Grounding

Grounding is possibly the most important single issue which indigos face.

Grounding means being connected with physicality and the Earth. It means being centred, present, and in the moment. It means being practical and realistic, and having a sense of proportion. Grounded people live here and now, rather than in a fantasy world.

In terms of chakras, grounding means being connected to the first chakra (and to a lesser extent to the second and third). The first chakra is an energy center located at the base of your body, around the genitals/anus.

In case you haven't heard of chakras or need a refresher, here is a basic map of the chakras:

1st chakra
Colour: red
Groundedness, physicality, security, stability, sexuality, our animal aspect

2nd chakra

Colour: orange
Sexuality, sensuality, emotions, pleasure, creativity

3rd chakra
Colour: yellow
Strength, power, protection, purpose, motivation

4th chakra
Colour: green
Love, compassion, forgiveness, connectedness, sociality

5th chakraColour: blue
Communication, expression

6th chakra
Colour: purple or indigo

Perception, intuition, insight, psychic abilities

7th chakra
Colour: white or violet
Spiritual connection, enlightenment, oneness

As you can see, the higher chakras deal with more ethereal stuff like perception, truth, and spiritual connection. The lower chakras deal with more Earth oriented stuff, such as power, sexuality, and survival.

The tendency of most Wanderers is to have their energy higher up in the body. Wanderers tend to value higher-chakra qualities more than lower-chakra qualities, perhaps even disdaining the lower ones. By keeping their energy higher up, they are more able to disconnect from the real world and live in a fantasy world, one that is perhaps more comfortable for them.

Here is an exercise that I've suggested to more than one indigo. First, sit in a comfortable alert position. Now, simply locate your energy or sense of self, and try and pull it down into the body. Pull it all the way down until your spirit's first chakra is connected to your body's first chakra; till you're completely anchored in the body.

This will almost certainly feel uncomfortable. In fact, you might not be able to do it fully, or you might not be able to maintain that state.

This exercise will probably not be enough to make you grounded in itself. Initially, what I want you to learn from this exercise is what grounding feels like. Once you get past the discomfort you associate with it, being grounded isn't a negative feeling. It's like sobering up. Try and see past the discomfort and just feel the groundedness itself.

The second thing this exercise is good for is for uncovering this sense of resistance you have in yourself to being grounded. Observe it. Be curious about it. Isn't it funny that you have this instinctual need not to inhabit your body?

Inquire into this need. Ask yourself, what purpose is this resistance attempting to serve?

It is through self-inquiry that you might unravel the knot which is your desire to stay ungrounded. I suppose your answers might look a bit like this:

*- I've been through too much pain in this life and I'm too sensitive to deal with it, so I prefer to disassociate with reality to avoid confronting the pain head on.

- This world is too awful, so I prefer to disassociate from reality to avoid it.

- I dislike physical stuff because it seems like the most crude, awful people focus on physical stuff. I identify more with people who see beyond that and have a more spiritual existence.* (Note: the physical and the spiritual are in reality not in conflict with each other!)

*- I don't feel like part of this world.

- This world moves too slowly, I'm not used to this rhythm and it's hard to match myself to it.

- My spiritual energy is too big and my body seems a poor fit for it.

- My passion is spirituality, so I don't have time for physical stuff.*

All of these issues need to be faced and resolved if you want to make any progress with getting grounded.

I think a good basic technique is to practice the exercise above frequently. Attempt to hold your energy in your body. Experience the resistance that comes up, and attempt to address it, one issue at a time. Repeat frequently, so long as you still feel resistance to being grounded. Note that this process goes deep, and while you should experience some helpful results quite quickly, completing the process will likely take years.

Do You Want To Become Grounded

This is the basic technique. However, in order to make any progress at all, you need to answer this question: Do you *want* to become grounded?

To start with, you probably *don't* want to become grounded. Not really. That's why you have the problem in the first place. Ungroundedness pulls at you while groundedness repels you. Why would you want something that initially feels so wrong?

I can - and will, in following - give you good, rational reasons. But beyond the rational, you need to find a way of wanting this with your heart. If you don't, then you'll never get anywhere; you'll just keep sabotaging yourself.

A universally healing practice which happens to have a lot of value here is the simple act of observation. Eckhart Tolle's The Power Of Now (an essential book for any Wanderer) explains this basic technique.

In meditation, you can grow in the quality of Presence by attempting to watch your thoughts or your breathing without judgment. When you have learnt to do that, attempt to bring this same Presence to your everyday life, watching the actions you engage in impartially. When you can do that, you start to gain some perspective on things, and behaviours that initially seemed to make sense might take on a different meaning.

I slowly discovered that ungroundedness was wrong for me by observing my behaviour. Again and again, I was screwing myself over by being impractical, by ignoring money or my physical needs, by putting the spiritual before everything else. I went through immense discomfort this way. Spiritually, I didn't gain much, because it is hard to really focus on spiritual stuff when you always have problems to deal with. It felt like the Universe was constantly slapping me in the face to get me to wake up and realise what I was doing.

I observed that my escapism didn't help me. It felt good and comfortable on the surface, but by taking more perspective I came to associate it with the pain of this *backlash* that the Universe kept sending my way. I came to realise that I didn't like feeling dizzy and disconnected. That was a disempowering feeling. It was a bit like being drunk; there are some payoffs that might make it seem worth it, but ultimately you're simply reducing your capacity to function.

Ultimately, I discovered that groundedness - my first chakra - was a part of who I was. Every chakra has a true and valuable function, and disconnecting from my first chakra was like voluntarily cutting my arm off.

A New Philosophy

It helped, I think, to learn a new philosophy. Previously, I thought that spiritual stuff was the only thing that was really valuable, perhaps influenced by Buddhist or Hindu ideas of "escaping" the wheel of reincarnation by becoming spiritually immaculate. In these perspectives, the world is a hindrance to spiritual realisation, and exists only to be transcended, not as an end in itself.

Eventually, I came to the intuition that God didn't make all this just to distract us from Enlightenment. This world is too big, too magical, to serve an absurd purpose like that. The world is here for a reason. We are here for a reason.

I agree that we all need to advance spiritually, but I don't believe that this is so that we can escape the world: I think it's so that we can finally enjoy the world like it was supposed to be enjoyed. When we all become spiritually advanced, that won't be the end; that will be the beginning.

As an indigo, I also believe that my soul comes from a world where people are already spiritually advanced. This messes with the "escaping" idea even more. I didn't come to this planet to escape it; I volunteered to give up paradise in order to help this planet evolve. It would be a gross misunderstanding of my purpose here if I were to live as a meditating hermit. Like all indigos, I have an individual life purpose I can feel in my bones. And life purposes, by nature, involve interacting with the world. You can't have a purpose that doesn't involve being someone and doing something.

Why Groundedness Is Important

Besides that, groundedness is important for so many reasons:

- You can't find your life purpose without grounding. As I mentioned, purposes involve interacting with the world, and if you don't want to interact with the world you'll never have access to that intuition that tells you what to do next. Without grounding, you likely feel lost and don't know what to do.

- Groundedness helps you think practically, be more focused, have a clear head, and get stuff done. It pretty much makes you smarter.

- Groundedness gives you power. You might have immense spiritual energy, but if you can't channel that through your body, it doesn't mean anything on this plane. If you want to be a powerful manifestor, then you need to be grounded. If you want to have personal "presence" and influence people, you need to be grounded. If you want to use your spiritual power to succeed with your life goals, you need to be grounded. A powerful soul without a physical tether is toothless.

- Groundedness will help you deal with your excess sensitivity and empathy. If you can stay anchored to your body, you won't lose yourself in other people's energies. Groundedness also allows energies to flow through you into the ground, as with a lightening rod. This prevents other people's emotions - or your own - from getting stuck in your aura and messing you up. It significantly increases the amount of stimulation you can deal with without getting overwhelmed. It also helps you to control your emotional state.

- If you want to advance spiritually, one way is actually through the body (e.g. Eckhart Tolle's inner body meditation). I believe that groundedness is actually an important - possibly essential - part of spiritual growth, even if you can be initially scared of it being the opposite.

- Having your spiritual energy housed in your body has a lot of benefits.

One, it nourishes and strengthens your body, preventing illnesses.

Two, it means that energy vampires can't feed off of you with such ease; these are for example the people who bring drama into your life so that you will lose your centre and bleed energy, which they use to feed their egoes. Show them that you're no longer an easy target and they will leave you alone.

Three, it means that you won't manifest wildly. Manifesting wildly is when your energy goes out in every direction, and you manifest positive situations and negative situations depending on your current state. Sometimes, life can seem like a bad dream, when you get stuck in a rut of manifesting endless negative situations. When you get grounded, you finally get the reigns of your manifesting power, and control what you are creating.

- Finally, I'd say that there is an intrinsic value to physical life, just as there is an intrinsic value to this Earth, which doesn't exist just as a foil for our spiritual development. The first chakra is 1/7 of all of you, and that's a considerable amount. Grounding is important because it is who you are.

The Work Begins

Now, after a period of self-questioning, hopefully you will discover that you truly do want to become grounded, despite an instinctual resistance you no longer personally identify with. Great! Then the work begins.

Do the exercise I mentioned above frequently. Try to hold yourself within your body as much as possible. Observe the resistance this brings up, and work through each point of resistance in turn. Make life your therapy room; the situations that come up naturally in your life may hold keys to your personal evolution.

Another exercise I find very useful is to stand with your feet firmly on the ground, and hold your hands down near your pelvic area, palms facing upwards. Then, pull them upwards, and at the same time breathe in, visualising Earth energy coming up into your body. I often use this exercise when I need a quick reminder of Earth energy, or when I want to ground myself before a ritual.

It can also be helpful to visualise your chakras. I was once told by a psychic that I should reduce the size of my chakras so that they were contained inside my body. While I had an initial feeling of resistance to this - I'm so much bigger than this lousy body! - it started to feel good. After all, when my energy was much more expansive than my body, it was outside of my realm of control, and was easily absorbed by energy vampires or just mixed randomly with other people's energy. I felt less vulnerable this way, in the end.

A similar exercise could be to feel into your aura and see what your energy looks like right now. If it's too expansive or beyond your realm of control, pull it in a bit. Try and make sure that your energy is housed in your body. This should hopefully be something you can do intuitively.

The Rhythm Of The World

Another important aspect of grounding is to learn to match the rhythm of the world.

As I mentioned before, Wanderers have a fast internal rhythm. Some call them "highly strung". This world, for them, goes far too slowly, as they instinctually remember a world where reality responded to intention practically instantly.

I have found that I become much more powerful when I learn to slow down my internal rhythm. I simply feel into my body and locate my rhythm, and intentionally slow it down. Actually, I simultaneously feel the rhythm of the world; the intention I put out is to make the two synch. I want to feel like I am taking part in the world, that my actions and the world's "actions" are happening at the same rhythm.

I find that as you slow down, you become more able to affect the world with your intention, simply because you are acting on the same plane as that which you want to affect. Accordingly, your world seems to speed up to meet you somewhere in the middle. An indigo's life can move much faster, much more intensely, than an average person's life. You can accomplish huge amounts in a very short amount of time, and Earth-shaking life events seem to come into your life with stunning frequency. In my case, the last three years of my life have felt like a decade each.

Physical Life

Apart from all this, just learn to appreciate physical life. Learn to see physical life as more of an end in itself, rather than simply a means to the end of more spirituality. Let physical and spiritual coexist and mingle, and not be exclusive with one another.

Learn to appreciate home, peace, stability and security. The ungrounded want to fly, are scared of landing. Remember that you can land and then fly again. The Earth nurtures you. She is your friend, not your enemy. Learn to love the Earth.

Learn to forgive this world for its immense cruelty. First see things as they are, including the extortion system which is our "economy", then let them find their own natural level of importance in your world view, one where you hopefully don't have to think about them every day. Create a bubble around you where things are more like they'd be in *Indigo World*. Then, hopefully the harshness of the world won't be so great that you need to fly away spiritually from it.

It can be helpful to do activities that involve your body. Exercise is great; especially, I find, exercise which you can engage in rather than exercise that is so boring that you just drift off. I started playing football (soccer) a while back, for instance, and I've found that the effect is so grounding that I sometimes feel like I get a new perspective on life after playing. Other grounding activities could be physical work such as cleaning or building or cooking.

I've heard sex is grounding, too. As far as I'm concerned, it's certainly helped me feel more like I want to be involved with this physical plane.

On Power

One aspect of being indigo is being, or feeling, powerful.

In our Indigo Worlds, reality responded to intention faster than here. There was more energy out there, and more energy in us. We remember a time when it was possible to do magic.

Nowadays, we still carry that high energy frequency of where we came from. We somehow *know* inside that we carry this huge power, and that what we choose to make reality, can become reality.

I believe actualising this power has a lot to do with grounding, and synchronising yourself with this vibrational reality. Through escapism, we subconsciously want to go back to that reality where we felt most at home. However, escapism doesn't allow us to deal with this reality very well.

When you've synched up with this reality, become grounded and practical and patient enough to work with the pace of things here, you can manifest your power within the parameters that this reality sets for us. That is, you're unlikely to start flying or throwing fireballs, but your determination, inspiration, intuition and inner strength will allow you to go far in the goals that you set yourself. And if you align yourself with the world's intention to grow in spirituality and compassion, you can become a powerful agent for change.

Possible with ways downtime is spent

But does your soul still long for REAL magic? I know mine does, which is why I guess it might in your case too. Well, I've sort of resigned myself to not being able to throw fireballs. Still, there might be some mind-over-matter stuff which *is* accessible to us. For instance, a quick look online will give you ample instruction on how to develop telekinesis*, even if those abilities will likely be meagre compared to the immensity of power you feel within yourself.

*e.g. the psipog.net archives; this link will redirect you: www.sophiagubb.com/h .

Then there is the actual practice of magic(k). Magick (the optional "k" is added to help distinguish from stage magic) could be roughly what many of us are looking for; the ability to affect reality directly using only our internal power and intention. However, so far I've never met a practitioner who was able to throw fireballs. Actually, the only time I really got into magic, I was rather unhinged and the concept only served to unhinge me further. It didn't help that many magic practitioners seem to be unhinged as well, and I was figuratively standing on the shoulder of giants in my pursuit of the loss of sanity and coherence. (You can read about this in my autobiography, Stubborn Soul: www.sophiagubb.com/stubborn-soul).

60

I, personally, have rather a fear of the concept of magick. Thinking about it too long makes me dizzy, reminding me of the days when common sense eluded me, and I felt like I was teetering over the edge of a precipice.

While I suppose Wanderers would have a natural ability at magic if they put their mind to it, I believe that the weirder aspects of this tradition resonate detrimentally with our escapist tendencies. If you ever want to get into magick, I would suggest only doing it after some years developing your skill in groundedness like a diligent little monk. This may sound horribly boring, but if you want to try it the other way round and face the consequences, be my guest.

Actually, I believe that the essence of magick is intention-manifestation, that is, putting into practice the understanding that reality is malleable and responds in some way to our thoughts, energy and intentions. As far as I've seen, the members of the intention-manifestation community tend not to teeter on the edge of madness in the same way as some magick practitioners do, and hence, it's probably a safer way of approaching what is essentially the same thing.

Intention-Manifestation

Intention-manifestation is the skill of affecting reality directly, outside of the realm of typical cause and effect.

One well known IM practice is the simple act of prayer. Those who engage in this practice often find out personally that it really works, and scientific studies have for example proven the power of prayer to heal, even at a distance and without the awareness of the ones being prayed for.

Generally, I don't favour prayer too much because it seems to depend on the power of an outside force (usually God[ess], Source, the Universe, etc). It feels more empowering to me to depend on an internal source of power.

Another fairly well-known form of intention-manifestation is the Law of Attraction. This term was coined by Abraham-Hicks (the collective of spirits that goes by the name of Abraham, and the channeller Esther Hicks). I've read some of their books, though I find them too complex and cerebral: and I have the sense that reaching an intuitive, not mental understanding is the key to the exercise.

What worked for me was a simple article from Steve Pavlina, called How To Order. (Quick redirect: www.sophiagubb.com/i). The basic concept of the article is, the Universe brings you what you desire; you simply need to ask for it, politely, specifically, and confidently. Imagine you are at a restaurant. To get what you want, you simply have to decide what you would like, and ask for it. It seems perfectly reasonable, but the surprising thing is how few people actually do this.

If you're unsure about what you want, the waiter will say, "OK, I'll come back when you know what you want." If you keep changing your order, then your meal will never come, because each time you make a new order, the cooks have to start from scratch again.

Don't keep repeating your order. The waitress already heard you the first time. Just be confident that you are going to be served. If you keep repeating the same order over and over, that also has the effect of resetting the process. So be patient.

Outside Forces

You might notice that this method includes some kind of deference to outside forces, despite me saying above that I prefer to depend on my internal source of power. Well, to be exact, I find that it resonates most with me to involve myself both with internal and external sources of power, and to understand that ultimately, there is no boundary between the two. Let me explain.

For me, intention-manifestation depends on the understanding that the Universe is a sort of dream. It only exists because we, as manifestations of consciousness, are dreaming it into existence. Who are "we"? Well, we are not our bodies, because our bodies are part of the dream too. We are consciousness. ← *interesting view although differing from mine personally*

Ultimately, if you follow consciousness back to its source, you always arrive in the same place: God(dess). So ultimately, God(dess) is what we are.

With this understanding, there are no external or internal sources of power; it's all one. I find it makes sense to me to immerse myself in that truth as I cast an intention.

In Practice

In practice, this is how I practice intention-manifestation:

First, I identify a desire.

Then, I access my power. This is almost second-nature to me by now, but for beginners I can recommend the *rooting technique* as described on page ***. Combined with the strength that wells up from the Earth, know your own internal power and your connection to All That Is. Then, cast your intention; it can be wordless, or in the form of a present-tense phrase, such as "A highly compatible, emotionally mature romantic partner is coming into my life". As your intention goes out, you might be able to feel a wave of energy flowing out from you into the Universe.

From then on, simply maintain a sense of expectant confidence. The intention you cast *will* come to you, in its own perfect time.

The interesting thing is that this process becomes a sort of conversation with the Universe. What you asked for will come to you, and then you will have to decide, "Was this really what I wanted? Do I want something else?". With each desire that is fulfilled, your future desires evolve.

Sometimes your intention might have only been only partially fulfilled when you realise it's not what you want. That's fine; you can take advantage of the fact that casting a new intention for something resets the old one, and cast a new, adjusted intention.

The Universe will also bring you feedback in the form of transformational experiences. If you desire something that you're not yet a perfect fit for, then you will need to change into the person who is able to have what you desire. For instance, if you desire a million dollars but ultimately wouldn't really feel comfortable being a millionaire, then in order to receive your desire the Universe will have to help you transform (It's a fact that most people who win the lottery lose their money soon after - they weren't really a fit for it, so it slipped away). Or, perhaps, the Universe will help you learn that you don't really desire it in the first place. Either way, the feedback you get from the Universe might make it seem to you like the Universe is not really doing its job. In actuality, it is only doing exactly what you need it to do.

Exercises For Integrating Your Power

Now, I want to outline a few exercises for integrating your internal power.

Firstly, false modesty is a big enemy here. Try to see yourself neither as more than you are (arrogance) or less than you are (false modesty); instead, try to see yourself as you really are.

If false modesty has consistently stopped you from coming to terms with your own power, then you will need to face up to that. Try for a moment to compare yourself to others consciously. After all, it doesn't do to dwell on your difference from others, but you still do need to know where you fit into this world, so a bit of comparison is necessary in its proper place and time.

You will probably feel resistance, either the urge to be more than others or the fear of being more. Try to observe these tendencies, and allow them to be there without, for once, influencing you. Over time, if you continue observing and working on these tendencies, you will learn to see yourself as you are.

Another exercise is as follows. First, feel into your aura. Notice its size, its intensity. Notice the feeling of purpose you harbour inside; notice the sense that you will achieve what you are meant to do. It's like confidence, but confidence can be deflated, so maybe not that; call it just, a knowing.

Now, you might notice a disconnect between your power and your body. Perhaps your aura seems too big to fit into this puny body, too expansive. Perhaps you just noticed that your soul is not rooted in the body, and not all of the spiritual energy is reaching it.

I believe that we often shut down our power for a reason. If you can't control your power it will go out into the world uncontrolled, creating wild emotions, conflicts, and manifestations. In this case, it becomes best to disconnect from your power entirely, which is what happens.

Supposing you have become more grounded and more aware of what you are doing with your power - or are willing to learn how to control it better - you can take steps to reconnect your power with your body. You won't be able to hold a power level you can't handle for long anyway, so there's not much of a risk. (If it turns out that you can't deal with your own power, work on grounding, self healing and generally becoming more adept at dealing with energy before trying this again).

Simply attempt to draw your expansive energy into your body. Feel it nourishing your cells, reconnecting with you. Heal the disconnect.

As I was working on this, I intuitively felt like doing a visualisation, which I will describe:

I sat down with my hands placed near my crossed legs and the fingers overlapping each other, creating a half-sphere shaped hollow. In that hollow, I saw a ball of red light appear, representing my first chakra. Then, red lightening came down from above, through all my chakras and into the ball of red light. I saw this again and again; each lightening stroke seemed to help bring my soul's power more in alignment with my body. At the end of this, I felt stronger, and a lot more *solid* somehow.

On Psychic Abilities

I've been told by various psychics that I myself am "very psychic" and I just needed to develop my latent abilities. So far, actually, I haven't developed my abilities to a very interesting point. My psychic attunement has come and gone over time, depending on how much I've worked on it; I've had a few cool experiences, but even more moments where I thought I was being psychic but wasn't, sometimes embarrassing myself. Perhaps because of my disappointment, I decided to leave off further study until a time when I could focus on it more intensively.

I've heard some indigos have a much easier time of it, growing up with clearly psychic gifts, such as talking to their spirit guides and predicting events. I wonder if my lack of ability is simply because I grew up in an atheist-skeptic household, and felt very pressured not to believe in or demonstrate any paranormal abilities.

Whatever the reason, though, it's clear that Wanderers in general come in a great variety of levels of ability as far as psi is concerned. Not manifesting much ability doesn't make you less of an indigo, though presumably there is some latent ability in you, supposing you choose to work on bringing it out.

A few tips I can give from my own forays into developing my psychic abilities:

1. Beware of false psychics.

The first psychic I went to, Erin Pavlina, was simply amazing, which was great for me but inadvertently caused me to have very high expectations for other psychics. I'd say that 90% of the psychics I went to were frauds or simply bad. One particularly awful one actively seemed to want to hurt me, for example by making up horrible stories about my then-girlfriend in an apparent attempt to destroy our relationship.

The remaining 10% were worth it, though.

2. Beware of *being* a false psychic.

Nowadays I usually try to practice my psychic abilities on things that I can confirm. That's because it's so easy to fool yourself into thinking that you are being a good psychic. After all, psychic impressions come from a very similar place in the mind to imagination, and it's so easy to get the two confused. Learn what a healthy level of confidence should be for your level of ability.

3. Reaching a good level of attunement may require becoming kind of ungrounded for a while, but learning groundedness in your daily life is still useful.

4. Try Mindfulness meditation in the style of Eckhart Tolle.

5. Being psychic and having a good intuition are largely the same thing, and sometimes it can be really helpful to shut your mind off and see how you *feel* about a matter. Or, if you can't shut your mind off, give yourself space: let a question sit in your mind for a time while you do other things, or go for a walk. Inspiration has a way of coming into spaces if you leave them open.

While I can't say I'm an impressive psychic, I believe that I've often been able to access my guidance when I've needed to - and that has definitely improved my life greatly. It's sort of a matter of feeling a bit more than thinking, and stepping into the flow of life rather than trying to control every step of the way. When you do this, things tend to fall into place as if of their own accord.

On Sex

They say that indigos are often either very sexual and sexually expressive, or not sexual at all, preferring to eschew sexuality for spiritual gain.

Wanderers can have a special relationship with sex, given that they are not easily controlled by shame or taboos. Some even capitalise on this and become sex workers, taking advantage of the fact that Earth people simultaneously desire sex and attempt to restrict its access.

I would like to go down on record here by saying that I don't believe there is anything unspiritual about sex. You don't have to do especially spiritual, tantric, meditative, etc. sex in order to make sex okay. Sex already is okay as it is.

I've seen a meme floating around Facebook a few times which says that when you have sex with someone their aura sticks onto your aura and stays there for seven years. I would very much like to emphasise: that is bullshit. I've fucked so many people that I'd be schizophrenic now if that was so. Quite the contrary, regular sex, including sex with a variety of partners, has had the effect of significantly improving my mental, and I think spiritual, health.

An indigo will not enjoy mechanical, disconnected sex. But it's not a case of choosing between marrying someone or having robot sex. Actually, I've found that I often have emotional and even spiritual connections with my casual sex partners. The real only difference from romantic partners is just that: they are casual. But the connection is real.

I'm not here to say you definitely should have sex in the same way I do, but I do want it to be clear that what I do is an option.

Non Monogamy

Related to this is the matter of ethical non-monogamy, a concept which is often used interchangeably with the similar one of polyamory. I consider myself polyamorous or "poly" because I know I can be in love with more than one person at the same time, and I feel no need to repress that by limiting myself to only one person. In turn, I see no reason to limit the relationships of my partners.

Wanderers often become poly, either because their tendency to love easily and powerfully makes it hard to ignore that they love multiple people, or because they simply want to question yet another social structure which was foisted upon them without explanation and which they think they can improve upon. I know that in my case, it was my desire to have a coherent belief system that led me to polyamory. As far as I could tell, there just wasn't a good justification for limiting my partner and myself.

Nowadays I am more aware of the problem of jealousy and I do understand that because of jealousy it can make sense to be monogamous as a conscious decision to avoid discomfort. That said, I believe jealousy comes from negative internal states such as fear and possessiveness, and spiritually speaking, it's good to work through that if possible.

This book isn't big enough to explain everything about polyamory, so I recommend searching on Google or Amazon for more information. For now, I wanted to throw that out there, and potentially stimulate further research.

LGBT

And while we're on the topic of sexuality, we should mention LGBT topics. I happen to be transgender and bisexual myself, which puts me in a good position to talk about it.

I believe indigos are somewhat more likely to be LGBT than other groups. I seemed to confirm this with a quick survey on an indigo adults Facebook group, where about 39% of 33 respondents were homosexual/bisexual as opposed to approx. 10% of the general population (to be exact, 27% of respondents were bisexual and 12% homosexual). In addition, another survey I made regarding gender identity only garnered five responses but out of those two (40%) were transgender, specifically gender-fluid. I'm sure my methods are a little crude so scientifically speaking, I wouldn't put too much weight on these findings, but it does seem to confirm my general feeling about Wanderers.

The question is, what does this mean? It could simply mean that indigos are more likely to admit that they are LGBT, or to realise it, than non-indigos. Seeing as indigos aren't influenced by taboos in the same way as other people, this seems like it is pretty likely to be part of the reason.

Another thing is that I think Wanderers, at their stage of evolution, having experienced many lifetimes living in many different ways, are multifaceted creatures, and tend to blend aspects which are traditionally expected to be confined to one gender or another. Some indigos also have past life memories, and if we accept that the veil between lives is thinner in their case, it would be logical that they would be more likely to be transgender if their previous life was as a different physical sex than their current one.

Finally, as I mentioned at the beginning of this book, Wanderers have a tendency to go through intense hardships in their lives which seem to serve the purpose of shaking them awake. These hardships are often illnesses, accidents, and disabilities, and while these might not seem to have much in common with simply being able to fall in love with different sorts of people, it's true that being LGBT often has the effect of shaking up someone's life, often drastically. At the very least, it forces you to look for different sources of social approval and to develop a non-conformist attitude in general.

Being transgender is a special case. I believe that even as there are considerably more bisexual, gay and lesbian Wanderers, there are *very much more* transgender Wanderers as compared to the general population. It may just be because I'm one and therefore resonate with them and attract them into my life, but I know rather many. This is despite it being a combination you'd expect to be rare in an objective sense. One Wanderer I know even came out and transitioned after having met me, partly inspired by my example. (We met before either of us had discovered our natures in this regard).

Being trans offers a special chance for spiritual growth. I find it gives me very special insights into the nature of gender as well as that of male and female social conditioning, insights which I try to share with others. As I found being socialised as male particularly restrictive, I'm interested in teaching men about gender socialisation coming from my unique perspective. In this way, I believe I will help evolve consciousness in this society.

Going into a full explanation of being transgender is beyond the scope of this book, but I will say a couple of things. Firstly is that if you happen to be both transgender and indigo, be careful to avoid burnout. I went through my gender transition as only an indigo would, with fiery warrior energy. My coming out was like the D-day beach landing. Yet transition is a marathon and not a sprint, and I ended my first year of transition drastically exhausted and depleted of energy. Don't burn yourself out.

One more thing I will add is not to let misguided spirituality get in the way of being yourself. I've seen two Wanderers who I was certain were transgender from the way they described their feelings to me, yet both of them resisted who they were, giving spiritual justifications. They both seemed to think that they just needed to learn to become comfortable with the gender typical of their physical sex, and that this was some kind of spiritual lesson they were going through.

Personally, I think a much more interesting spiritual lesson is learning to accept oneself - and yes, being transgender is a part of who someone is - and coming to terms with the nature of gender. I also really don't think that anyone just "grows out of" being transgender, no matter how spiritual they are. Lots of therapists have tried to do that for people and failed.

Don't let your spirituality turn you into a fundamentalist Catholic in disguise. Often the spiritual scene gives us wisdom that sounds fresh but is nothing but repackaged traditional prejudices. Question everything; you know how.

On Home

One key to understanding your nature as a Wanderer is to understand where you came from.

As I've mentioned before, the definition of an indigo is someone who is not from here; someone who is from a better place. That usually involves previous incarnations in a planet of light, one where people have reached a point in their evolution where love and compassion is just normal, and the everyday callousness of Earth a thing of the past. It can also mean other things: perhaps you previously existed as an angel or other being of light who hasn't even incarnated. Or perhaps you had another existence entirely. However, at the very least it means that you have come from an existence of light.

This is, of course, the explanation for the feeling that you are not "from here". You literally aren't. A lot of indigos don't quite understand this feeling and often go from one place to the next looking for the place where they will feel at home. The trouble is, that place does not exist on Earth. Unless you recognise this fact, and grieve appropriately, you may end up in an endless loop where you never find roots for yourself.

Of course, moving can be good - sometimes essential. A Wanderer needs to find people who will understand and accept them, and chances are that this will be easier in a larger city where there are more alternative "scenes" to choose from. Some places are also just more leftist/liberal and alternative than others, and hence, you're likely to feel more comfortable there (as well as having a better chance to find people who are like you).

But if you find yourself relocating again and again without finding a place to put down roots, it might be good to question your motives. Are you looking for something that you just can't find here on Earth? Are you in denial about what Earth is like?

I believe there is a cure to this horrible homesickness. It is twofold:

One part of the cure is to come to terms with WHY you are here. You didn't come here to have a holiday - that is for sure. And you also didn't come here to "learn". What could you learn from such a cruel planet? How to be cruel? How to deal with cruel people? The first thing is not something you'd want to learn, and the second thing is only useful if you're on this planet, making the logic a little circular.

Indigos came to this planet to help create change. As the Law of One states, in a discussion about Wanderers:

> *[An entity] may conclude that its desire is [to serve] others [by] reaching their hand, figuratively, to any entities who call for aid. ... These entities are from all reaches of the infinite creation and are bound together by the desire to serve [here]. ... The desire to serve [involves] a great deal of purity of mind and what you may call foolhardiness or bravery, depending [on your point of view]. *

So, you have come here to help. Come to terms with that. I think when you take a long term perspective, one lifetime in relative discomfort on this planet is not too hard to deal with if it's for the sake of a larger mission. You can, of course, rest in the Ether or perhaps in "holiday" lifetimes on other planets* in between doing your work here. It's something you can look forward to, and the knowledge that you are not doomed to such a dark place as Earth *but came here by your own choice* - even if it is a choice you don't remember making - can make this feel less unbearable or hopeless. This is not your home. You're just making a foray.

*I assume this, though I don't see why it wouldn't be possible.

76

The second part of the cure to Wanderer homesickness is to make a little bubble of "home" around yourself. Surround yourself with friends and chosen family who feel like home. Immerse yourself in daily activities that feel like home. Minimise your involvement, as far as possible, with the dark side of Earth. By that I don't mean not to help out when you can, but just, don't get involved in the games which dark Earth society tries to drag you into. This may be hard to start with - indeed, constructing a life which works for an indigo is a major project, requiring time and dedication - but finally, you can succeed, and this can give you some measure of inner peace.

In order to achieve an existence that is largely detached from the dark side of Earth, you will have to make peace with the darkness here. That is, stop raging against it. The more you fight darkness with darkness, the bigger the darkness will grow. Instead, disengage with the darkness as much as possible. Walk away from dark situations. Walk away from standard school, standard work, dark family and friends. This may not always be possible, of course, but when you're stuck raging against these things you may not see just how possible it is.

If you simply can't walk away from something, though, attempt to react towards it as little as possible. Regard it as an annoyance, a little itch that you do your best to ignore. Then, focus your energies as fully as possible on healthy things, things that feel like home. Even if you are in prison you can still meditate. Find the positive thing you can pour your energies into.

You Are Different

Seeing as you're not from this Earth, you find the cruelty here both hard to understand and hard to fully get your head around. I find that especially younger or less realised indigos tend to assume that Earth people are nicer than they are. Perhaps they stubbornly refuse to see that people are violent, simply because seeing this reality would cause them to despair. Yet, until they can learn to see Earth people as they are, they're easy victims, and keep getting screwed over again and again.

It helps to understand that you are different. Embrace that reality. Learning that this world is cruel is a sort of loss of innocence. You might never be as carefree as before, but you will be a lot more mature and able to respond to the harsh reality you find yourself in.

Money

Seeing as you're not from this Earth, you probably also find the concept of money bewildering (as I've previously touched on). In the place of light where you are from, money is not needed, as everyone supports each other freely.

You may long for communism or a gift economy, and perhaps even try and bring that about. In my opinion, this is not the best use of our energies right now. Just because you know how the world would be better doesn't mean we have to try and go directly to that vision without stopping anywhere in-between.

Understand that it is not money, nor any other system that makes the world dark. It is simply the fact that people have violence in themselves. We may reduce that violence by improving the system, or we may improve the system by reducing that violence. The two do support each other, but we can't advance too far with one while still neglecting the other. If we just dropped Earth people into a gift economy right now, they wouldn't know what to do with it, and would mostly revert to the old ways soon enough. On the other hand, if we could get all Earth people to evolve sufficiently, a change in system, and therefore a revolution, would be necessary. Ultimately, I believe it's the internal, spiritual change which is most important, and I prioritise it over the structural change. If people change internally, the structural change will follow.

Don't mix up your longing for home with your spiritual mission. You can't change the world enough in this lifetime to feel at home here, so don't even try. Instead, try to support the flow towards spiritual evolution that already exists.

Relationships

Seeing as you are not from this Earth, you may find relationships a little confusing. Before I began to surround myself with people who were like me, I found that few people could understand the innocence and purity of my love. (This sounds rather arrogant to my ears that have been subject to Earth social conditioning, but I trust you can see past that to the meaning I intend to impart). I would almost always love more intensely than the other person in my relationships, and yet would also have a rather different understanding of love. For others, love seemed to mean possession, yet for me, it was an energy that flowed from me and which wasn't limited to one person or one means of expression.

I have often had to explain that when I say "I love you", it doesn't mean what others expect it to mean. It doesn't necessarily mean that I'm attempting to sign a relationship contract. I doesn't necessarily imply future of any sort. All it really means, is that in that moment, I am feeling love.

Wanderers want to love just as much as they want to be loved, if not more. This brings them to an unusual problem; Earth people find it hard to be loved. They have some kind of limit beyond which they either can't understand or simply can't accept a certain level of love. This hurts the indigo, who feels a great welling of energy that has nowhere to go.

Ultimately, I think the only solution is to find people like you, who are able to understand your love. As you improve your ability to find like-minded souls, this will become easier just as many other things will.

PART FOUR: UNDERSTANDING YOUR PLACE IN THE WORLD

Am I Crazy Or Is The World Crazy?

Wanderers often find themselves having this question: "Am I crazy or is the world crazy?"

The answer: the world is crazy. But let me elaborate.

While we Wanderers have very clear instincts about how things should be, it's often the case that no-one around us seems to see what we see, and this can create a social pressure which makes it really hard to trust our instincts. Over time, we can even cave in and start believing what society is pressuring us to believe.

Sometimes what we see can seem SO OBVIOUS to us. To us, it doesn't even need an explanation, just as pointing to the sky and saying "it's cloudy" doesn't need an explanation. We just see it. But when the entire rest of the world is walking around telling us that it is not cloudy but is, in fact, a sunny day, it seems natural to wonder if it is we, and not them, who are hallucinating.

We might ask ourselves, who are we to think we are so special? Isn't it kind of egotistical to think that I am the only person in the world who sees things as they are?

Well maybe it is slightly ;) Others ARE out there; you simply haven't met them. And believe me, when you finally get to talk to such a person, it is SUCH a relief. Perhaps reading this book is that relief for you, right now.

I think there are two reasons why it is hard to accept that the world is crazy. One is that we resist thinking of ourselves as special. The other is that seeing things to be as shitty as they are would be too much to deal with. We can't accept it, and would rather seek solace in denial.

On Being Special

One of the Wanderer's biggest issues when waking up and learning about themselves in relation to the world is seeing themselves as special.

Obviously, if you accept that you are unique and much more evolved than most people on Earth, that can be a horrible ego trap. Most Wanderers sense that trap before falling in it, though, and are just left with the problem of how to avoid it while still seeing themselves clearly.

I dealt with this issue by tentatively trying on the indigo label for size, and kind of cycling between distancing myself from it and getting closer to it in order to progressively deal with the ego issues that came up. I always attempted to try and see things as they were, and see through the illusion of ego.

Sometimes, it was empowering for me to say, "Yeah, I'm more evolved than most of the people on Earth, so what??". Sometimes it was empowering for me, in my writing, to take on the role of an arrogant person. It was hard to express what I thought was true without feeling arrogant, so I just surrendered to feeling arrogant for a while. Later, it became easier to state what sort of person I was without using an arrogant tone.

Actually, eventually, it became less important for me to state who I was in this way, and less important for me to compare myself to others in terms of evolution in the first place. Nowadays, I pretty much never think about how I compare to others, though if you brought up the topic I'd still have an opinion.

What helped most was surrounding myself with people who I could connect to, and avoiding "normal" people like the plague. There came a point where I didn't think about "normal" or "evolved" people anymore. The "normal" people were off my radar, not so much of an influence in my life any more.

By being satisfied with the people I surround myself with, and being confirmed in my points of view rather than feeling like I am crazy, I no longer worry about being different. I am now a "normal" person in my little bubble of people who the rest of Earth society would consider very abnormal indeed.

It helped me go through a period of realising I was special, though, and coming to terms with that. A principle of the spiritual discipline of Alchemy states: *before conjunction comes separation*. You split apart in order to come back together again, in a more harmonious configuration than before.

If I hadn't had my phase of separating from society, I might never have found my true place. Indigos who refuse to believe they are special often spend years or lifetimes living a life of denial, hanging out with "normal" people and doing "normal" jobs which don't nurture who they are. You have to realise you are different in order to be able to honour yourself.

Admitting The World Is Shitty

A related subject is admitting the world is shitty.

In spiritual circles, we're very much encouraged not to be negative. We're supposed to see the beauty in the world, and the goodness in people, and not see everything as shitty.

The thing is, you can look at the world in either way. You can see it as shitty, or you can see it as beautiful, and in both cases you can find valid reasons why you are right. In the end, neither perspective has ultimate truth. As with many such dichotomies, the reality is a bit of both.

And I do agree with the truth that focusing on the good in the world is a very healthy and spiritually sound thing to do. I admit I could do more work on that. But I believe it's most important first of all to see things as they are.

Indigos have a tendency to view the world as shitty because, unlike most people, they have in their instincts the memory of a better world. Indigos actually have a point of reference, and can actually have some kind of objectivity when saying whether Earth is a nice place or not.

And we know that compared to *Indigo World*, Earth is a horrible, horrible place.

It is a nightmare.

The things that go on here every day... and not just the big horrible things which everyone can agree are bad, like war or torture... what about the everyday horrible things which most Earth people don't even notice? The institutionalised soul crushing which happens everyday in school as children are broken down to function in a hierarchy. The continual humiliation in jobs where an employee must follow nonsensical rules in order to stroke the ego of their superiors, so that they don't have to face the threat of ending up on the street. The unforgivingness of a world which forces you to jump through hoops in order to "earn" your basic rights.

Deep in our soul, this tortures us. We *know* it's all wrong. And okay, in spiritual terms perhaps nothing is "wrong"... in which case, how about cruel, uncaring, inhumane.

Yes, the world is full of wonderful things, but cruelty is *institutionalised* here on Earth. You have to work hard or be lucky to build a life for yourself where you simply aren't treated like expendable trash on a daily basis. If you have to *work* not to get treated like trash, I think we can objectively say that Earth is a shitty place.

Now, just as I no longer think about how I compare to others in terms of evolution, I no longer spend time thinking about how the world is shitty. I had my phase. I needed to come to terms with that.

It didn't help that there were very few people I could talk to who understood. "Spiritual" people tended to think that there was something very wrong with me taking this perspective, and often talked down to me trying to get me to see the light. Other people just couldn't understand my otherworldly viewpoint.

Despite doubting myself, as we do when it's hard to find someone who understands us, I did manage to fully process my understanding of the shittiness of this world. It depressed me for a while, even. Then I got out of it.

Nowadays, if you ask me if the world is shitty on an objective scale, then I will say yes. However, I just don't really think about it anymore. On a day to day basis, I don't need to make an evaluation of the world either way; I'm just not dealing with the entire world.

And I have my friends and lovers who form this little indigo bubble around me, letting me feel like everything is alright. So for me, my world is great. Not Earth, no, Earth is not great, but my little world within Earth, yes.

In Denial

Alternatively, you may be in denial about how shitty the world is. This can result in a kind of naiveté where you expect others to be kind and reasonable and then get taken advantage of, because they are not.

For most Wanderers, I find, this is a phase. It soon enough gets replaced by a bitter stage of realising just how crappy the world really is. I think this is good, because after *that* you can finally move into a balanced worldview.

But some indigos may be more resistant than others. They want to cling to the thought that humans are good, kind, compassionate. The thought that they might not be is horrifying.

Obviously, deluding yourself is never healthy. And when you've noticed you're deluding yourself, it's not really possible to continue anyway. But it might help a bit to try and find a nuanced, empathic view of human darkness. People vary a lot - so there are kind, compassionate people, yes. Most of the rest have some amount of compassion and a varying amount of dysfunction that blocks their compassion. Some are sociopaths and have no compassion.

The trick is to avoid judging people as good or bad, but instead try to see them as they are. You may not always understand their reasons for acting unkindly, but you might be able to remember that there are always reasons, no matter how twisted, and from a certain perspective those reasons make sense.

You might also simply need to come to terms with the fact that you are not on the planet where you originated. (See: Home ***). It's an uncomfortable thing to consider, but you need to get used to it and make the best of the situation.

You're Different

Learning to understand that you're different - not even necessarily special right now but different - is so important. Again, you might have resistance to feeling that you're different because it feels like being arrogant. But you need to see yourself as you are.

Indigos who don't accept that they are different often fall again and again for the trap of trying to do things like "normal" people do. That can involve working in a "normal" job even though it kills their soul, forcing themselves to accept hierarchy even though it feels like death to them, or forcing themselves to go to loud parties even if they don't like them.

You need self understanding. Hopefully this book can give you that. You also need to accept yourself the way you are. Accept your feelings and needs, even though they are unusual and most people can't understand them or help you feel affirmed in them. Accept that you need to live differently to other people.

The life of a fully realised indigo is radical. She or he has a radical way of earning money, a radical lifestyle, a radical mission. She or he spends time with radically unusual people.

The only way you can flourish as a Wanderer is with a lifestyle that others consider radical.

Because of this, you can't afford to try and blend in. If you do this for an extended period of time, the crying of your soul will *crush* you.

If you have extended periods of depression, consider that it's probably because you need to make changes to your life, changes which you haven't felt brave enough to make yet. Depression is this crying of your soul. No matter how much you fool yourself that things may be okay as they are, your soul knows better.

Not feeling brave enough to make a change is okay. Accept that and don't beat yourself up about it. But consider that it is literally a matter of life or death that you take steps to eventually create a life that allows you to flourish. You can't live under this depression forever. If you don't feel brave enough now, leave it for a while and wait until the resources you need come to you.

Living radically will require losing friends. It will require burning bridges. This world isn't really made for people like us. We need to kind of repurpose the things we find in our environment into working in our favour. It's like taking a kitchen tool and using it for garage work. But with a bit of creativity, we can get it to work out.

On Conspiracy Theories

It's fairly common for Wanderers to get into conspiracy theories.

I won't beat about the bush: I'm not a fan of most of what can be considered conspiracy theories.

Let's see... I suppose it's quite reasonable to assume that aliens exist and are simply being covered up, or are covering themselves up to quarantine Earth from their influence. However I haven't seen any evidence to absolutely convince me of that.

However:

AIDS is not an invention. I mean, *seriously*. (I recognise that this is not an actual argument).

The Earth is not hollow. Study some physics.

Jewish people don't control a particularly large amount of the world's wealth. You can confirm that by looking at who owns the Fortune 500 companies. And even if they did... is there any reason other than anti-semitism to actually care?

Chemicals in the water are not making people gay. If that were possible, a significant number of people would make themselves gay in order to piss off Christian fundamentalists and avoid unwanted pregnancies. I'd make myself straight and then queer again just to make myself like, extra queer.

Obviously, if you believe in conspiracy theories I can't do much to sway you. I mean, conspiracy theories in general are overwhelmingly anti-semitic and LGBT-phobic, and I could appeal to you on those grounds. But I guess if you're deep enough into this stuff you'll have an answer to that (which I do hope is not "fuck Jews and LGBT people!").

Why Wanderers Are Drawn To Conspiracy Theories

I think conspiracy theories are particularly attractive to Wanderers because they do sense a kind of negative force in society. It's true the modern school system was designed in order to acclimatise children to hierarchy. It's true that much of politics serves the interest of a wealthy few. It's true that pharmaceutical companies encourage people to die if that's what's more profitable.

Once you get into that, I suppose there's a certain seductiveness about going further. Imagining bigger, more powerful enemies generates fear, and fear, in turn, expands the vividness of the enemy you imagine. The more powerful your enemy, the more "informed" you feel you have to be in order to protect yourself. In other words, it's a spiral. You become paranoid, cynical, and dare I say... unhappy?

We've already gone over this a bit. The world IS shitty when viewed through the eyes of a space traveller, but you have to process that information and find where it fits into your wider worldview. Not everything is shitty. Life doesn't have to be shitty. More importantly, there's no value on focusing on the shittiness past a certain point.

In the same way, there's no value in focusing on enemies (the Rothschilds, the lizard people) past a certain point. If you can't change things, then who it was who did a certain shitty thing to society doesn't really matter. And, in fact, if you *can* change things, the information probably doesn't matter either.

I think a healthier view of reality is to understand that society has been formed by people of varying intentions, some kind and some malicious. Malicious people might coordinate their efforts with each other for mutual benefit, but I feel this happens less than some think, simply because they aren't team players by nature. I also believe that malicious people are less intelligent and less powerful than many give them credit for. They operate much of the time from a kind of animalistic consciousness, trying to get what they want if they can get away with it. The sad fact is that a lot of humanity's ills come not from evil per se, but stupidity and apathy. And perhaps selfishness, but not a megalomaniac selfishness, more a kind of "if I don't see who I hurt then it didn't happen" short sightedness.

The short version is that fear causes your perception of real or alleged dark forces to expand. Letting go of fear and operating from a place of "I focus on what I have influence over" reduces that vision, and reveals a more complex picture, an interplay of many different forces on a wide spectrum of discordance and harmony. It's perhaps a little disappointing, because if there's no big enemy then there's no way you can play the hero. But I think it's still a much more pleasant, and particularly, *effective* way of viewing the world.

On Family

There's a lot to say on the topic of family for Wanderers.

Many, if not most, Wanderers feel very estranged from their blood family. The reason is simple: there are a lot more indigos trying to incarnate right now than there are indigos to be their parents, so most new Wanderers need to incarnate in non-Wanderer families.

This is very hard for most indigos. Non-Wanderer parents are not usually sensitive to a Wanderer's needs, indeed are not usually sensitive to a human's needs, or a soul's needs. The form of parenting which Earth society teaches as normal is very toxic. Children are treated with punishments and rewards, often hit or beaten, and stringently controlled. Parenting without manipulation, hierarchy or violence is considered "radical" on Earth. (Google: Radical Unschooling).

This causes a huge trauma in Wanderers; perhaps even more so than in Earth people, because Wanderers are more sensitive, especially in childhood, and react more violently against imposed hierarchy. They may become very estranged from their parents and even disown them.

I'm not sure how much wisdom I can give on this because I still feel like I'm going through a process, mostly involving learning to forgive my father for beating me. (Perhaps forgiveness is a tricky word; "letting go" of it might be more accurate).

In practical terms, however: find some way of living independently as soon as possible. This may be hard, especially as it can be very hard for indigos to adapt to Earth's economic system, but it's really, really important if you're living in a toxic situation. If you're still a child and are legally not allowed to live alone: may I suggest beginning already to develop a skill which will help you pay for your own place to live? Computer programming being what I would suggest to my past self if I ever took a time machine to visit her.

If you've succeeded in living independently then naturally your parents will have less influence over you. At this point, all you need to know is that it is your choice how much of a place your parents will have in your life. Sure, it might be a bit harsh to cut off contact, or limit contact very stringently, but if contact makes you feel bad, don't make yourself sick just for your parents' sake. I won't say that you have NO responsibility for your parents' feelings - it's a balancing act as with everything - but your life is your life, and your parents do not have ownership over it.

It may also be useful to take a "time out" where you remove your parents' influence so that you can develop yourself independently, and become more independent, before you expose yourself to them again. This can be an indefinite time out or one with a well-defined limit, or something in between. It's generally kindest, emotionally speaking, to communicate what you know about the length of time as best you can.

You've depended on your parents in varying degrees for much of your life, but what can be easy to miss is that they need* you too. So, try to be gentle, is what I'm saying.

*If you need to cut off contact entirely, though, they can certainly live without you.

The one good thing, however, about having gone through the harsh experience of growing up with Earth parents is that you might be able to save other souls from that experience. By which I mean: when you have children, they will most likely be Wanderers themselves.

Of the Wanderer parents I've known, almost all have had Wanderer children. The only exception I know of is that of a very bitter, angry Wanderer who never made peace with existence on Earth. I strongly suspect that her violent, angry children - clearly Earth souls - were drawn to her energetic vibration. All I can say is, take care of how you manifest.

Actually, in most cases, it seems that children born to Wanderers are of a *higher* vibration than their parents. This is because the higher vibration you are, the harder it is to withstand negativity. Some souls simply would not be able to incarnate here on Earth without a Wanderer as their parent, or would be psychologically immensely damaged from doing so. Wanderer parents are in demand by such souls.

In terms of "indigo" and "crystal", this means that an indigo parent is likely to have a crystal child.
Crystal children rely on the energetic protection of their indigo parents. They take shelter in their parents' auras, avoiding venturing further if they are in a public or otherwise unsafe place.

Anecdotally, I've also heard that just as indigo parents have crystal children, crystal parents are likely to have "rainbow" children. According to The Internet, rainbow children are beings of such high vibration that they simply cannot experience negative situations; negativity simply bounces off them, or exists as if on another plane. Hence, it's not that incarnating to negative parents would hurt them - it's that they simply cannot do it in the first place.

Whatever the specifics of your situation, I'm certain that having Wanderer children and giving them the shelter they need to develop fully is a very worthy life purpose. The second generation Wanderers can hit the ground running, engaging with their own life purposes without having to spend years on healing first.

On Being A Lightworker

As a Wanderer, you will feel the urge to make some positive change in this world you live in. It's the very reason your soul chose to incarnate here. This means that, while free will still exists, you probably just can't feel really fulfilled unless you accept this aspect of yourself and attempt to make good on it.

Those who take up a mission to help this world advance in its spiritual growth are called lightworkers. Not all lightworkers are indigos, but a pretty large proportion of them are. All indigos feel the calling to become lightworkers.

Feeling the calling is not the same as being a realised lightworker, however. You will need to spend some time grappling with the calling and coming to terms with it; and you will need to make a conscious choice to accept it (-- or not - free will again).

I went through this process myself when I was about 18, and beginning to find myself. I had read Steve Pavlina's thoughts on the topic, and it made me think: *how shall I orient my life? What will be important for me?*

Ultimately, I came to understand that this life felt meaningless if I wasn't assisting in the positive evolution of this world. I went through little depressions (Dark Nights of the Soul) where small parts of me died; old self-serving goals became suddenly uninteresting to me and disappeared. Everything felt hollow unless it fit in to my larger purpose.

When you start aligning yourself with the lightworker path, you soon discover that it's not quite how you expected it to look. For instance, I had decided that I was going to dedicate my life to assisting the positive evolution of this world, but I couldn't just start doing my inspirational speeches or writing books or running NGOs or whatever else. I was still living in financial instability, bogged down with emotional issues and personal troubles. I had to deal with all of that stuff first.

As of this writing, at age 25, I still live a life which is largely oriented towards self-care. I discovered slowly and painfully that just securing a stable existence on this Earth was not as easy as my alien soul expected it to be. I was also forced to face up to some extensive personal issues in the realm of self-love, which were blocking my progress at every turn.

I understand that even though I am doing these unglamourous, self-oriented things, the lightworking is in the context. Through my self-care now, I am building myself a life where I will be able to serve fully in the future. And my self-understanding as a lightworker helps: it gives me a source of motivation for moving forward, a motivation I couldn't have accessed otherwise.

Darkworkers

Note that the opposite of a lightworker would be a darkworker - a being of extreme selfishness. An indigo would rarely become a darkworker unless they happened to become saturated with pain. Reaching such a level of pain is just about possible, and an indigo darkworker must be a terrifying sight. Yet, the lightworker calling is so strong in us that I think most would simply kill themselves before becoming so completely controlled by pain.

Circling round the internet is another definition of darkworker, a rather confusing philosophy which suggests that you can be both *dark* and *good* at the same time. I believe that the problem here is that someone decided to equate the occult *Left Hand Path* philosophy with darkworking, which by logic must then be the opposite of lightworking. This logic doesn't really work.

The Left Hand Path philosophy is one that rejects religious authority and social taboos, and suggests an elevated focus on the self. Due to the first two aspects of it, I believe it may be attractive to indigos, especially those who are just beginning to find the strength to push back against society's domination. The last aspect of it is not too beneficial for those who would want to embrace a lightworker path.

Being a lightworker is not the opposite of the Left Hand Path, hence, you can reject religious authority and social taboos as a lightworker (and I would encourage you to). In the same vein, if you want to experiment with a dark aesthetic, just remember that it doesn't have to get in the way of your desire to assist the world in its spiritual evolution.

Misconceptions

When you're beginning to grapple with a lightworker identity, there are a lot of misconceptions which I think have to be addressed. For instance, a lot of people would assume that a lightworker would look like a typical do-gooder or a saint, but honestly, those archetypes are twisted by what society thinks is "good", which rather involves submission and not rocking the boat. Jesus of Nazareth was crucified for what he did. I would rather like to think that if I eventually get crucified for doing what I do, I can consider that a sign that I did something right.

Another way I think people get confused about lightworkers is thinking that it's all about helping people. While that's close enough, I think it's more helpful to see it as "assisting the spiritual evolution of the world". Just *helping* a person may help them evolve, by showing them what kindness and compassion looks like. Then again, it may not.

I often think about this when considering activism that seems to involve "battle". For instance, I was once involved with some students who were struggling against University reform by aggressively squatting a University building.

I'm in two minds here sometimes, as I can't always say that "battle" is wrong. Sometimes the social changes created won through fighting lay a fertile ground for people to develop spiritually. However, I believe it might also be often counter-productive, spiritually speaking. Battle doesn't help people to learn to be compassionate. It doesn't help people to open their minds to new ideas. Usually, it does the opposite; people's hearts shut down, and their minds close too. Who wants to listen to someone who is attacking you? In the end, perhaps you'll win a battle, but from the wider perspective, you're harming the greater cause. Injustice is created by violence, and unless we can remove violence from the hearts of people, injustice will continue. Viewed this way, using violence to further our ends is questionable at best.

I also think about this in my work for animal rights. There's been talk recently about laboratory-grown meat, which would hopefully be cheaper than slaughtered meat and hence reduce the demand for slaughtered meat. Yet, I think that so long as people don't learn to feel compassion for animals, this solution won't help that much. If times changed again later and people had an opportunity to kill more animals again, they would do so, in an instant. Only an internal, spiritual advancement will ever be truly meaningful if we are to end suffering in the long term.

It's kind of a "give a person a fish, and they will eat for a day" problem. Give a person compassion, and they will have light for a day. Teach a person compassion, and they will have light for eternity.

Service To Others

Another misconception is that lightworking is about *service to others*. While this is again roughly true, it misses out a few key points. Firstly is that self-care is often incredibly important for the overall mission of a lightworker, as I mentioned above. Secondly, I believe that being a lightworker means not really making so much of a distinction between *self* and *others*; in fact, that's kind of the point. By breaking down this barrier we appreciate all people, including ourselves, as part of the larger body of humanity and of creation. That's why we feel such an urge to contribute to the whole.

Therefore, I would define lightworking not as *service to others* but *serving the Whole of which you are only a part*. When we're serving the Whole, we serve ourselves too, cause we are part of that Whole. Actually, we need to serve ourselves a lot, because the responsibility for fulfilling our basic needs comes down to us. If you've ever observed a parent caring for a child, then you know that an individual has a lot of needs that need fulfilling. If we don't fully care for ourselves, then we may require others to help us, which drains their resources. The only way to serve the whole is to serve yourself fully, and then work outwards from there.

The Best Path

I believe that ultimately the best path for a lightworker is to serve themselves and the greater Whole through the same means as much as possible; that is, to find profitable work which will earn them money and serve the greater Whole at the same time, or else to find non-profit work which will inspire others to support them financially while they do it. The key point here is that working a standard 8-hour job leaves little energy for other things. Your spiritual mission should be what you do full-time.

It's not "unspiritual" to ask for money for your work. You don't have to take a typical view of money as a way of satisfying your own greed. You can instead simply view money as a way of empowering you to do more of your work. Ultimately, you will give more than you take. And you can still give away free work sometimes to combat economic inequality, when you see that that is appropriate.

Spiritual Perspective

One thing that separates a lightworker from just any activist is their spiritual perspective. They know that they are not just working to change society, but to go to the root of social injustice, which is the violence that people carry in their hearts. They understand that there is already a flow bringing humanity towards this sort of spiritual evolution, and that they simply need to be a part of this flow.

I find that my understanding of reincarnation helps me a lot. It gives me a longer-term view. Activists tend to be a despairing lot, always bobbed up and down by the wins and losses of their generation. As far as I'm concerned, the outcome of one battle or another isn't such a big deal. The question is, how will things look in a thousand years? A long term view makes things feel more optimistic, and also makes me feel more empowered. Change can and will happen in that timescale, and little things like such and such a law or such and such a corporate injustice won't make such a difference overall.

I also don't feel too bogged down by the fact that there is so much darkness in the world. My understanding of my nature as a Wanderer gives me a bit of distance; I'm here in this world as a volunteer, not a prisoner. As well as that, most people compare things subjectively, to how things were or how things should be according to them; but as an indigo, I have some kind of objective measure to compare things against -- my instinctual memory of the world I came from. I know that according to that objective measure, this world is horribly violent and cruel. Whatever changes happen in this generation will honestly not be too huge compared to the immensity of cruelty that already exists on this planet every day.

I also think that it's important for a lightworker to understand the difference between "changing the world" and "assisting the world in its spiritual evolution". While I do sometimes talk about "changing the world" out of convenience, I think that strictly speaking, the phrase has a bit of arrogance in it that needs to be avoided. "Changing" something without its consent is violent. Asides from going against free will, it suggests that you are moulding things in your vision of what is good, which may not be actually what is needed. On the other hand, if you assist something in its evolution, you are acting consensually, and non-violently.

If you despair that the world is wrong and needs changing, just realise that every person, no matter how lost, carries the instinct towards spiritual evolution in them. Even on the animal level, they avoid pain and seek pleasure, and developing spiritually would lead them to greater fulfillment, if only they realised it.

Some people are ready for change, and these people will seek you out. Therefore, you can simply orient your work to supporting those who are seeking change. As those people change, they will provide a stronger structure to encourage other people to change, and so on. It's perhaps a slower process than you might like, but the wonderful thing about it is that it works, and it is working. It has been working for a long time. Just join this pre-existing flow, and you can add your strength to it.

Finding Your Purpose

So, you've decided that you want to walk the lightworker path. Now how do you find your purpose, your individual spiritual mission?

This is a question that I hear a lot when counselling indigos. It's not an easy question to answer; I myself spent a very long time struggling with it. I tried to get answers from psychics, but none of them were very satisfying. Kristen Finlayson once wrote:

Unfortunately, not many sources outside of yourself can tell you exactly what you are supposed to be doing. In the process of discovering your purpose you discover your "soul self" or who your higher energy is (guide, angel, etc). So this is a bit of a lonely journey of the soul. Some people can tell you that you are supposed to be a healer or that you are an Earth Angel but not much beyond that. That is because the guides want us to discover this for ourselves. In doing this we then can help others in the process of discovering themselves. Plus, as Indigos we don't like people telling us what to do...so you wouldn't really listen if someone did give you the answer anyway.

Steve Pavlina recommended an exercise (sophiagubb.com/j) where you sit yourself down and try to write down what you think your purpose might be, letting your feelings guide you so that every iteration gets a little closer. Then, finally, your life purpose is the one that makes you cry.

Maybe I just wasn't that connected with my emotions back then, but when I did the exercise I couldn't find anything that would make me cry. I did find something that I still believe has meaning for me: "To find and express the Sacred Truth" -- The Sacred Truth being a term I invented for the core of meaning, the essence of things, that which remains when you burn away all that is meaningless.

Yet, interestingly, discovering this seemingly meaningful factoid about myself didn't actually change anything. I still felt lost, adrift in life. Such an abstract answer did very little to give me a practical path of action.

Looking back, I see the search for purpose not so much as the search for an answer, at least not the sort of answer that you can write down in a journalling session. I see it more as a work of self-transformation, where you finally become the sort of person who is connected with their internal sense of purpose.

I believe grounding is absolutely key here (as it is for so many things in a Wanderer's life). This is for the simple reason that your life purpose takes place in physical reality. If you're disconnected from physical reality, you're disconnected from where your purpose is.

For me, purpose doesn't necessarily mean a grand vision. It basically means knowing what to do next. Then, when I have done that thing, I find myself in a new present moment, and again, I know what to do next. I don't *necessarily* know what that second thing is while I'm doing the first thing.

When I'm connected to my purpose, I feel a sense of drive. I don't feel lost. I know I'm going in the right direction. I can feel this way even if I only know what I have to do right now, and have faith that afterwards my next step will become clear to me.

How does my current life purpose look? Well, as I write this book, I know that I have to lay a foundation for my future work. I have a relatively vague idea about what my future work will be; I will be expressing my creative energy, an energy that I feel inside me begging to be released. I know that energy is positive, and will help the world. I simply trust in it.

That said, I can imagine that I will be writing books, doing workshops and talks, and campaigning for things that matter to me. I can think of many specific things I will do when I've laid my foundation, but I am not overly attached to any of them. I am certain that when I reach that stage things will become clearer, and that whatever specific thing resonates with me the strongest in the moment will be what I end up doing.

What is my foundation? Well, I need to create financial stability for myself, preferably by earning money from things that contribute positively to the world. I also need to develop in self love, something which relatively recently I discovered was holding me back in every aspect of my life, not least the financial.

Right now, I'm getting used to my new cooking job while trying to find a new place to live (quite an effort in Berlin sadly). I'm trying my best to rest and recover from several rough emotional blows life has dealt me. I'm also writing this book, obviously.

If you look at my plans, they get progressively vaguer the further into the future you go, and are very specific in the present moment and for the next few steps. It's good to have a general idea of where I'm going, but it's only in the present moment where I need to REALLY know what to do.

Doing Things

When I was trying to discover my purpose (or my sense of purpose, as it turned out), I found myself drawn to *doing things*. I started my blog when I was eighteen, dizzy, lost, and with no better idea of my purpose than 1. survive and 2. save the world. I had the idea that my blog would help me with both of those things.

I later jumped between occupations: voluntary hobo - vegan cook - reiki practitioner - raw food guru - English (as a second language) teacher. Each step seemed to bring me somehow a little closer to my sense of purpose. Well, none of them were quite right for me, but what they did do was help me realise what I wanted and what I didn't want. They also helped me in my long process of coming down to Earth and becoming practical.

All this time, I kept writing my blog. After a year of reasonable success as a freelance English teacher, I began my gender transition - a life event that served to bring me much closer to who I was, and to ground me further. Within the next few months I also noticed that my motivation had become clearer; I really wanted to write. My blog, and future books, were to become a long term goal of mine. I felt driven like I had never felt before. This was *right* for me.

I think it was key simply to try things. The more I did that, the more I could learn to feel what resonated with me and what didn't. And learning to feel this also meant reconnecting with my core, with my essence, with my drive. This, in turn, allowed me to live with purpose in every moment, rather than just have a mental idea of what I thought my purpose was.

If you want to speed this process along, all I can say is, learn grounding. Re-read the chapter on grounding and do it, do it, do it.

PART FIVE: CARING FOR YOUR PARTICULAR NEEDS AS AN INDIGO

High Sensitivity

Unless you know alot, this book would be helpful to see that someone else out there believes in you and gets you.

Wanderers are highly sensitive. Not all highly sensitive people are Wanderers, but all Wanderers are highly sensitive. If you look for resources on Highly Sensitive People (HSP) you'll probably find something useful (and will likely stumble across the work of other indigos, whether they know about that label or not).

High Sensitivity means that intense stimuli can overload you and make you uncomfortable. I think it's very useful to come to terms with this, and adapt your lifestyle accordingly. Our society doesn't really cater to HSPs, so you have to make a special effort to find a lifestyle that works for you.

When I was younger I wasn't aware of my sensitivity, so I often ended up in packed and noisy environments, such as loud bars, parties, or discos, and found myself feeling stressed and uncomfortable. The trouble was, I stubbornly thought that I *should* enjoy these settings -- perhaps because I thought I needed to be social, and didn't know how else to accomplish this -- and tried to push through my resistance. This rarely resulted in anything positive.

The thing is, when no one else seems to have the same issues as you, it can sometimes be pretty hard to recognise the issue in yourself, or to take it seriously. After all, you have no role models in this area, no one to validate you in your experience, and so if you lack self-compassion (as I did) it's all too easy to downplay your difficulties or to brush them aside.

So let this book be that role model and give you that validation. *It's okay to be highly sensitive. It's okay not to like loud parties. It's okay to have special needs which other people don't have.*

Be kind to yourself and allow yourself to have different needs to others. If the "normal" way of socialising doesn't work for you, ask your friends to socialise with you in other ways, or find friends who prefer to socialise in other ways anyway.

I also find that it's really helpful for me to take little breaks when I'm overloaded. Sometimes I can still deal with - say - an intense party: I just need to "cool off" and then I can get back to the action. I either go for a walk alone, or I lock myself in the toilet for twenty minutes and mess around with my smartphone.

Grounding

Funnily enough, I find that I managed to take the edge off my extreme sensitivity by - you guessed it - grounding.

Grounding runs counter to your first impulse, because when you're overloaded by stimuli it's easy to want to escape into the ether. In these moments, your energetic body practically floats away; you feel that housing yourself in your own body is unbearable.

If you can push through the discomfort, though, and ground yourself fully, a funny thing happens: by being able to focus your energy in your body, it no longer flows outwards into the word of distracting stimuli. Your body becomes a refuge.

Psychic Gifts

There's another issue here; Wanderers are generally psychically and empathically gifted in one way or another, even if their abilities don't manifest in obvious ways.

Empathy, in particular, is worth discussing here. The psychic quality of empathy is the paranormal ability to feel what other people are feeling, even when they are not directly communicating those feelings with you. Those with this ability are called empaths.

When you're in a large crowd, and haven't learnt to control your latent empathic abilities, you may be feeling the feelings of everyone around you. Feelings are noisy and distracting, and besides, most people on Earth are pretty full of negativity, so this can get painful. The energies can jump into your body, and leave a residue that bogs you down for some time.

Again, grounding is key. The problem I've found with empathy is that when my spiritual energy doesn't have an anchor in my body, it jumps out wherever my attention goes. I sort of forget myself, and for a moment I "become" the person I'm perceiving. My energy mixes with the energy of other people, something which you can probably imagine is not very healthy.

If you can anchor yourself in your body, your energy won't go flying out all the time in this wild and unhealthy way. You will remember who you are and not "become" other people. And any energies you do pick up from others will discharge easily through your root chakra. If you are outside of your body, on the other hand, you won't have access to your root chakra in order to discharge like this.

Ekhart Tolle's inner body meditation helps here. I absolutely recommend his book, The Power of Now, to hear about it in his own words. (Also I absolutely recommend it as a spiritual book in general).

For now, I can give you a quick overview of the meditation:

Start by feeling into your hands. This is where the technique is easiest. As you place your energy and attention into your hands, you may notice a sort of tingling feeling within them. Focus your attention there deeply, and that feeling will begin to expand.

Now you can move your attention into your feet, and do the same. Then, do the same with your lips.

From there, move onto feeling the energy of your entire body. If you have been able to get this far, then every part of your body will have some tingling that you can access with your attention. Ultimately it will become one unified energy field. Rest in this field for as long as you feel comfortable, then ease out of the meditation.

This meditation has many benefits, but the one benefit for empaths in particular is that it helps you stay rooted in your body. You can still send your energy outwards and "read" other people, but if you can manage to have part of your energy still in your inner energy field while you do so, then other people's energy will effect you much less.

Diet

Much has been said on the internet about the "indigo optimal diet" (a term I found in the indigosociety.com forums).

Wanderers have a highly tuned system which tends to respond very sensitively to food and environmental stimuli. They are likely to have allergies and other sensitivities.

I believe like all people, indigos will vary in their specific needs. However, the internet seems to generally agree on these basic principles: reduce animal products, refined sugar, caffeine, and processed stuff in general.

This isn't something that you just "should" do because it's supposed to be healthy or something; many indigos report real improvements in their general wellbeing when they make these changes. It can be worth a try if you feel sluggish, depressed, irritable, or have a heavy digestion after meals. The right dietary adjustment can help with all sorts of issues such as these and more.

Besides the things already listed, it could be worth trying giving up gluten. Indigos have a propensity for allergies as I said, and gluten is, after all, one of the most common allergens that exist. I also get the impression that it is just hard on a sensitive system.

Veganism, of course, is the end result of removing all animal products from your diet. As well as the health benefits involved, veganism is worth your consideration if you consider compassion an important value to you. After all, there is no way to slit an animal's throat lovingly, and it's never kind to kill a cow's baby in order to take the milk intended for it.

If you want to learn about the dietary issues involved, I'd suggest you get on the internet and research the matter a bit. The short story is that you might want to take B12 supplements (though even that is not a guaranteed issue) and otherwise can basically just eat whatever you ate before, but replacing the animal products with some extra beans, grains, potatoes or tofu. Protein, calcium, iron, and so on are simply non-issues*.

I've also heard that a raw diet has a beneficial effect on many Wanderers. I myself found that it made me feel rather "floaty" and was probably not the best fit for me. It may be worth a try, however.

Give these all changes a go, together or separately, and see what effect they have on you. I would suggest that you keep them up for at least a month, as bodily changes can take a while to manifest (especially so in the case of gluten).

*To be exact, they might be issues, but not more so on a vegan diet than on a non-vegan diet. Barring a certain amount of randomness, if you ignored them before and were fine, ignoring them while vegan won't be worse than that.

Addictions

Indigos tend to have "addictive personalities". I believe this is because of their tendency to escapism and their need to dampen their sensitivity. It can be relatively easy for an indigo to become addicted to things like caffeine, sugar, or harder substances, which in turn has the effect of locking them into negative states.

Wanderers are not just likely to be affected by physical addictions. Other addictions can affect them too, such as addictions to Facebook, video games, or even spirituality. Yes, spirituality can become an addiction; anything you do in an unbalanced way and without self-control can be considered an addiction.

So, what to do about it? Well, developing in grounding will help you in learning moderation. If you are able, it may also help to simply attempt to avoid the object of your addiction and to give your body a chance to adapt to being without it. Afterwards it may be possible to return to a more balanced relationship with it.

If an addiction just won't budge, it may be that there is some pain in your life which you are trying to medicate. You may simply have to face up to the pain, and stop running from it. Change your life situation; break out of a toxic job or emotional environment. Or perhaps what you need to do is simply own up to some truth in yourself that you have been hiding from.

Sometimes, though, what you view as an addiction can actually be serving a positive purpose. Try inquiring into what purpose you are trying to fulfill with your addictive behaviour. When you know what it is, you might be able to fulfill that purpose in a healthier way. Or, you might even come to a different understanding of your behaviour and choose to see it as a positive thing.

Case in point: I have had a Facebook addiction for a long time. I recently realised, though, that Facebook can be essential for me when I'm dealing with intense emotions; it provides a necessary dampening effect, so that the pain doesn't all hit me at once. When I can, of course, I try to deal with them without this crutch, but I am very happy for the ability to slow down the emotional process and deal with things in my own time.

Interestingly, since I've come to understand the role Facebook plays in my life and have started working with it and not against it, I've felt freer from my addiction. In a way, it's not an addiction anymore, because I'm freely choosing to use it to serve my particular needs rather than falling into using it unconsciously. Some might say that the effect is the same, but I think the difference is significant. Besides, I now use Facebook less, perhaps because embracing the process in a conscious way allows that process to work more efficiently.

Handicaps and challenges

As has been mentioned before, Wanderers very frequently go through some kind of intense disease, handicap, accident or other life challenge. Some of these difficulties can be overcome - even those which you are told are impossible to overcome. Commonly, the difficulties happen early in life, while the indigo is "waking up", and disappear later. Sometimes, though, you may have to deal with your challenge forever.

When you are forced to deal with a devastating problem, it can be hard to find the meaning behind it. Indeed, sometimes I'm not sure whether we *should* look for a meaning behind it. Sometimes horrible stuff happens, and that's just how it is. Yet, how can it be that such intense experiences are so common for Wanderers, without there being some kind of meaning or reason behind that confluence?

If I can think of any reason why Wanderers so often have to suffer - asides from the fact that they are just sensitive and react more strongly to the negatively they encounter - I would guess it would be something about spiritual awakening. Intensely harsh experiences have a way of scouring the superficiality out of your brain, leaving you a deeper, more compassionate person. Intense suffering also helps you learn to live in the moment; the more you try to escape into your thoughts, the harder the pain becomes. At some point learning a Zen attitude becomes critical for your own sanity.

These lessons prepare you for your spiritual mission, making you both more able to heal the world and more determined to do so. After all, you made huge sacrifices in coming to this negative planet, and you did so in order to make a difference. It would suck immensely if you finished your lifetime, returned to the ether, and then realised that you had wasted your life in a cubicle job. In order to make your sacrifice worth it, you have a stronger need for intense waking up experiences than the average person.

If it's true that this is the reason indigos suffer, I can think of only one remedy for it: help the process along. Read Eckhart Tolle's *The Power Of Now* and attempt to live through your experience in a meditative manner. Let the suffering have its maximal effect, in the hopes that you will need less of it.

I'm sorry I can't give better advice than this. It kind of sucks being a Wanderer on Earth, but just remember that you chose to come here, even if you don't remember doing so, and from a higher perspective, it will be absolutely worth it -- even if it's hard to see that right now.

Another plus is that when a Wanderer overcomes their difficulties, they have a higher than usual capacity to experience peace and joy, as a sort of counterbalance to their propensity for suffering. I'm often glad I'm a Wanderer, knowing that my inner being is clean of much of the poison which passes for "well adjusted" in our society. And if I still have residual difficulties to overcome, I'm still happy at least in the knowledge of my great potential for future fulfillment.

Just keep in mind that these sorts of extreme difficulties normally manifest in childhood and young adulthood. Once you've overcome them, life will usually become much easier again, and you'll no longer have a much higher probability than others to have these sorts of experiences.

Crohn's Disease

I've already mentioned that one of my life challenges has been to be transgender. Actually, this wasn't the hardest. My biggest challenge, which fit very much into the Wanderer pattern, was Crohn's disease.

I had intense symptoms of Crohn's disease starting from when I was eleven till about the age of 21. At that point, it improved by 99%. A few minor symptoms remain, but the illness doesn't dominate my life like it used to.

It's sometimes awkward for me to describe Crohn's disease because some of it is rather "TMI". In short, however, I can say that I went through immense pain on a daily basis. This came and went to some extent, but much of my teenage life I really did not feel like I was living; I was simply pushing through.

I came close to death at one point, experiencing a level of pain that was so extreme I could barely think. I came back from that, and eventually had some kind of a life again, though it was only when I stumbled across the idea to give up gluten that I finally healed to the point where I am today. (I believe emotional healing also contributed to my physical improvement, but gluten had the most dramatic effects).

Crohn's disease taught me a sense of proportion in life. It helped me learn to focus on the big things and avoid getting bogged down by petty drama. I believe it hollowed me out in some way and gave me more space to develop compassion and peace. I also found that shortly after intense periods of pain, I'd have periods of spiritual bliss. I believe that the pain had forced me into small "ego deaths", which, while not permanent, gave me a taste of what inner realisation could be like - and that helped motivate me to attempt to find it again.

Depression

Depression is very common for indigos. I suppose that's pretty much to be expected, as we're sensitive, unique people with an urgent sense of purpose, and the environments we grow up in are usually not nurturing to such sensibilities. To feel better, we need to find positive surroundings and start living our purpose to some extent. In some way, this whole book is about doing just that, so I might not have too much to write in this section.

However, I can give you some basic tips for dealing with depression in a more immediate way.

Firstly, remember that things are likely to get better. Don't lose hope. Even if you feel alone, you have a team of spirit guides in the ether who are working non stop to help you find your way. If you're going through a Wanderer illness, remember it will likely vanish when you have learned the lesson it is trying to teach you. And if you are under 18 and stuck in toxic school and home environments, remember that life will get *so* much better when you become independent.

If you can't access your purpose now, channel your energy into something creative. Art, music, cooking... these will all help you feel less frustrated about not living your spiritual purpose.

Don't beat yourself up about being depressed. This is a good tip for anyone, not just Wanderers. If you can't do something, just accept that fact. Spend as much time in bed as you need to.

And, of course, do your very best to improve your environment if at all possible. If you can't right now, then just keep slogging through.

Existential Angst

Related to depression is existential angst or distress. Existential distress, as I understand it, comes from being disconnected to Source or the spiritual aspect of life. When you are finally able to feel that dimension on some level as a continuous presence, life stops seeming so meaningless.

How to get to that point if you're not already there? One tip I can give is - search if you feel compelled to search. Some said to me that giving up the search is the wisest thing to do. I ignored those people, and though the search brought me a lot of pain, the results were worth it.

Otherwise - I will recommend, again, Eckhart Tolle's work; it was ultimately what brought me to my answers. As well as this, I found that getting readings from good psychics to have a powerful effect in confirming for me the existence of other realms, on a feeling level as much as on a mental level. Besides this, if you fear death, challenge that fear. Look to where that fear leads. Beyond the fear of death is the sensation of immortality and with it, a connection to that which is immortal.

Another tip, as small as it may be, is that I found that the "meaning of life" came to me as a feeling or connection, and not necessarily as an answer that can be verbalised. At most, I can describe aspects of it - the social aspect of our existence, the flow of Universal intention, the channelling of creativity, the expression of Love... but the most important part is accessing that feeling. You have the answer when you feel that you no longer lack an answer. It doesn't have to be something you can speak aloud.

Suicidality

I hear that Wanderers are more likely to fail at suicide attempts than others. The Universe wants you here, and in fact, ultimately, YOU do too - just a part of you that you can't access right now. The gun jams, the rope breaks, you vomit up the pills.

Some Wanderers still do succeed, of course. So if you're considering suicide: don't. This is not just anyone telling you this, but a fellow Wanderer, so listen.

Things might feel horrible now, but imagine how you feel when you return to the ether and realise that you could have fixed things, that your negative state was only temporary, and that you had many great things that you intended to do while on Earth. That you had just messed up your OWN plans. And then, from your new perspective as a spirit in the Ether, you decide to try again, sending part of yourself down into what is quite likely to be just the same sort of mess as before.

If life feels intolerable now, try to remind yourself that later on, suffering seems like an illusion. By later on I don't just mean back in the ether - yes, that as well, but also from the perspective of your future, happy self. When you're out of suffering, it never seems as big or as weighty as when you're in it.

Another way of tackling this is a bit more technical. It has to do with Self Love. I do a lot of work on Self Love and have found that when I have suicidal feelings, self love often gets to the core of them. I realised at one point I couldn't love myself and want to kill myself at the same time. If you become your own ally, then the pain of the outside world becomes easier to cope with.

By the way, I'm not saying that suicide is never a valid option. It's just that that is very, very rarely the case. In a Wanderer's case it's even less of a good idea because there is so much you sacrificed just to be here. Try to have patience and keep working on changing things, no matter how much things suck right now. Trust me.

Chronic Anger

Chronic anger was a huge issue for me for a long time. It probably had a lot to do with being abused by my father as a child as well as never learning a good mechanism for dealing with anger. Besides this, it was also surely caused by specifically indigo issues: for example, that of having an internal sense of dignity which reacted violently with society's attempt to make me pliable. I also think a lot of it came from perceiving injustices in the world and feeling like I was alone in perceiving them, that the rest of the world wanted the status quo to continue and for me to shut up about it.

While searching through my emails I found some advice from Kristen Finlayson. I feel the urge to copy this paragraph in full because I think it was simply so perfectly expressed:

The anger is because of our uniqueness in a world and society that is literally like living in a septic tank. We are the kings and queens, used to flying, and feeling pure unimaginable love. Communicating telepathically and being invincible. So we are like fallen angels here but the kicker is that we fought to be here on a soul level. When we came into human form we forgot everything while still keeping the essence of who we are on a soul level. So we still feel powerful and important but this shitty world and everyone in it tells us otherwise. Here we are the freaks and the outcasts. Like changing a school where we were popular, happy, and loved to where we are being bullied and pushed aside.

It helped me a lot to simply get away from the sources of my anger: my father, my school, and potential hierarchical jobs. This, of course, required me growing up into an adult and being given the legal prerogative to live alone and earn money. Until then, I simply waited for that time to arrive, and even now I can't think of much better advice to give to people in that situation. Simply, hold on, I suppose.

Once I left those situations I needed to process my chronic anger. I tried to express my anger, in conversations and blog posts, and presumably that contributed to my anger slowly diffusing. It helped a lot to meet people who shared my points of view, and finally having the chance to express myself without feeling like I was crazy.

I spent a long time raging against the machine. I spent years doing things out of a place of resistance, out of hatred for the way the world works. For instance, I tried homelessness and squatting and all sorts of things to avoid doing "real work". These ended up hurting me a lot more than they hurt my imagined enemy.

I think it's a lot more healthy to live life from a positive place, rather than from a place of resistance. If everything you do is based on resistance, then what you are resisting will always have power over you.

That's not to say you should ignore injustice. My opinion is that anger is a sort of pointer towards a truth. You need to look past anger and not take anger as truth itself. Anger towards an injustice points towards a deep caring you have inside of you and a desire to help create a better, kinder world. Ideally, you can follow your anger to this positive place, then leave behind your anger, it having done its purpose.

I think you can perform this process on much or all of the anger which you experience as an indigo. Let it show you the positive message you've been ignoring. Sometimes the message is simply that you have to find a better environment. Sometimes the message is that you have a spiritual purpose you've been unaware of.

I also believe that, seeing as my anger brought me to some very self-destructive ways of living, one solution (which is the solution to so many things, I've found) may have been to work on self love. As it is, I'm coming to self love at a time when most of my chronic anger is resolved, so I can't test my hypothesis.

Explaining how to develop self love is beyond the scope of this book, but you can search my website sophiagubb.com for my writings on the topic, and perhaps I will write a book about it some day. I've placed a self-love meditation in the appendix of this book, which I hope may be as useful to you as it has been to me. Otherwise, simply make an intention for guidance on the topic to come to you.

On Awakening Spiritually

As a Wanderer, you will almost certainly have an intense desire to develop yourself spiritually. Even if you don't actually believe in the spiritual world, you will still have this desire; it will just manifest in an interest in wisdom and self-development. (That said, I suspect that most hardcore atheist-skeptics would have been scared away from this book by this point).

There is a lot to be gained from spiritual pursuits. Developing spiritually allows you to feel more positive, more at peace, suffer less, and generally feel better in the same situations as compared to before. It also allows you to develop your compassion and to be a positive healing influence on the world. Conversely, if you have untransformed negativity in you, it's possible that your attempts to change the world will backfire.

Even though Wanderers can become negative, they still have a powerfully positive core, and this, at least, does not change. This translates into a sort of natural aptitude for spiritual development. Therefore, a lot of spiritual development will be just remembering what you have developed in previous lives, and not exactly discovering anything new.

A lot of the advice in this book comes from my own life lessons, and accordingly, I feel compelled to warn you not to become too unbalanced in your pursuit of spirituality. If you read my autobiography, Stubborn Soul, you can get an impression of how that can happen. Basically, if you get obsessed with spirituality to the exclusion of everything else, that will end in trouble.

I suspect I wouldn't be the only indigo to have that problem. The trouble is, a lot of the books I read about spirituality seemed to make out spiritual "enlightenment" as being so incredibly valuable that everything else pales in comparison. My radical mind took that rather literally, and wanted to throw everything else away in order to focus single-mindedly on that goal.

When I was living like that, I hit brick wall after brick wall; it turned out I just could not advance spiritually without fixing some other aspects of my life. In fact, as I delved a bit deeper into this truth, I eventually came to consider that there isn't really a separation between my life and my spirituality in the first place. I could attain practical results in my life by developing my spirit, and my spirit would be nurtured by certain practical things. Indeed, the pursuit of economic stability - one of my biggest issues in life since leaving my parents' house - has led me down many paths of self-development, not least the development of self-love.

At some point, I basically decided to take some years to chill out about spirituality. I focused a lot on becoming grounded, and challenged and broke down my beliefs rather than building new ones.

In one of these purges I chose to eliminate the concept of "enlightenment". While I don't exactly disbelieve in it, I don't exactly believe in it either. Perhaps better said, I've simply set the concept aside.

In practical terms, I found the idea of enlightenment to really play into my ego. It's somehow the ultimate achievement, and hence, it's the ultimate desire of the ego; ironic given that it's actually supposed to mean the *death* of the ego. It also creates a separation between gurus who "have" something and the students who "don't have" it. I got the impression that so long as I wasn't enlightened, I couldn't really understand the gurus, and would therefore just have to take their words on some things. The obvious problem with that is that if you can't decide for yourself whose advice is worth following, you have no agency at all. It's the perfect setup for a submissive, disempowered religious situation, which was anathema for me.

Whatever the actual truth about enlightenment, I've come to accept that I can raise my spiritual vibration, and that that is good. Raising my vibration is the main goal of my spirituality. If enlightenment exists, I would expect it to appear somewhere down that path. With that in mind, I don't really need to focus on it. It will come up, or not, without the need for my intervention.

Breaking From The Standard Mould

There are other ways in which I broke from the standard mould of spiritual life. For instance, I came to believe that processing negative stuff was important, hence I largely rejected the "positive thinking" meme that is going around the spiritual scene these days. I also rejected that sexuality was unspiritual, or that a healthy amount of materialism was unspiritual. I rejected the idea that I had come here to "learn", knowing that my soul's mission was rather more outwardly oriented. I also rejected the idea that skepticism was a bad thing, and I made sure to filter my spiritual beliefs rigorously.

I guess what I want to say with this is that you can pick and choose what you believe in and how you're going to engage in spirituality. You have a powerful inner guide, so do listen to it. You'll be going off the beaten track, but that's just how you are, anyway.

The Power Of Now

I have already mentioned Eckhart Tolle's The Power of Now several times now, but seeing as we're on the topic of spirituality I'll take a moment to focus on it.

The Power of Now found me in a time when I was still more or less atheist, despite searching intensely for answers to my existential discord. The book contained brief mentions of more esoteric ideas, but most of it was very grounded and practical, and I was able to read it from my atheist position.

The thing is, it resonated with me in a way no other book had done. In moments of my life (such as after harsh episodes of Crohn's disease) I had experienced what I might call "existential joy" - being happy for no reason, feeling wonder at the beauty of the Universe; and as I read the book, I saw the essence of those moments reflected back at me. I felt the truth of the words deeply, in a way that went beyond reason alone. I soon understood that the book held the answers to my years-long search.

Some would say that Eckhart Tolle is just rehashing ancient wisdom for the modern age. This may be true, but actually I don't see anything wrong with that. Ancient wisdom, in my opinion, wasn't preserved very well (Jesus of Nazereth's words being finally put to writing almost a century after he died, for example), and even asides from that, the teachings were directed at people who have a different context to people today.

I certainly find that Eckhart Tolle resonates with me more powerfully than anything ancient I've read about. And quite aside from the words, I experience there to be a sort of spiritual energy *behind* the words, a vibration which helps guide you into higher states in and of itself.

Okay, I've said enough. Just go read it.

WHAT NOW?

OK, so you've reached the end of this book, what now? Well, just in case I didn't repeat this enough... get to work on grounding. Like *seriously*. I haven't even met you, but I know you need grounding work. Really, really do it.

And in general... just remember you're not alone. This planet may seem like a crazy place but you won't be here forever. (For me that's a comforting thought, anyway). Simply tune into your soul purpose and actualise it, and you can make meaning out of the painful fact of being here. And you can find others like you. When you do those things, things can actually start being fun.

Oh, and check out my blog at www.sophiagubb.com if you haven't already. I write about spirituality, personal development and social justice issues, all topics that I think Wanderers are very likely to be drawn to.

Good luck.

Appendix

Meditations

Breath Awareness Meditation

Breath awareness is the bread and butter of any effective spiritual practice. To engage in this practice, first find a position where you can feel alert and comfortable, set a timer for ten or twenty minutes. Close your eyes, and allow your focus to rest on your breath; either on the point where air enters and leaves your nose, or on the sensations of air moving through your body more generally. When you notice your attention straying from this focus, simply move it back there. To start with, you might get the impression that your mind is becoming more noisy and not less, but that's an illusion due to the fact that previously you simply didn't *notice* how noisy your mind was. Becoming aware of the noise is, in fact, progress.

After practicing this meditation enough you will move past the difficult beginnings and have the chance to experience some really cool states. Remember, however, to bring the energy of meditation into your real life as well. When you can, practice living in the moment, resting in your senses the same way as you rest on your breath in meditation.

The Inner Body Meditation

Start by feeling into your hands. This is where the technique is easiest. As you place your energy and attention into your hands, you may notice a sort of tingling feeling within them. Focus your attention there deeply, and that feeling will begin to expand.

Now you can move your attention into your feet, and do the same. Then, do the same with your lips.

From there, move onto feeling the energy of your entire body. If you have been able to get this far, then every part of your body will have some tingling that you can access with your attention. Ultimately it will become one unified energy field. Rest in this field for as long as you feel comfortable, then ease out of the meditation.

A Grounding Exercise

First, sit in a comfortable alert position. Now, simply locate your energy or sense of self, and try and pull it down into the body. Pull it all the way down until your spirit's first chakra is connected to your body's first chakra; till you're completely anchored in the body.

This will almost certainly feel uncomfortable. In fact, you might not be able to do it fully, or you might not be able to maintain that state.

This exercise will probably not be enough to make you grounded in itself. Initially, what I want you to learn from this exercise is what grounding feels like. Once you get past the discomfort you associate with it, being grounded isn't a negative feeling. It's like sobering up. Try and see past the discomfort and just feel the groundedness itself.

The second thing this exercise is good for is for uncovering this sense of resistance you have in yourself to being grounded. Observe it. Be curious about it. Isn't it funny that you have this instinctual need not to inhabit your body?

Inquire into this need. Ask yourself, what purpose is this resistance attempting to serve?

The Rooting Exercise

Stand with your feet firmly on the ground, and hold your hands down near your pelvic area, palms facing upwards. Then, pull them upwards, and at the same time breathe in, visualising Earth energy coming up into your body.

Self Love Exercises

I find it useful to "attack" the issue of self love from many angles. I start by asking myself what my current attitude is towards myself, and attempt to feel into my aura to see if there are any energies representing self hate. Knowing that these are created by me, I make the conscious choice to simply stop creating them, allowing them to fall away.

It's helpful to ask myself, "Am I being kind to myself right now?" and "How can I be kind to myself right now?". These questions help to expose self destructive behaviours and give me the chance to choose self-compassionate behaviours.

Finally, I find the *Self Love Meditation* extremely useful. I rest my awareness at the centre of my chest, and say: *"I love myself"*. These words create some kind of glow or warmth in this part of my body. With my intention, I make the feeling expand, and I attempt to bring it into every corner of my body.

If it's hard to find this glow, try to think back to when you had a crush or were in love with someone. This same feeling can be the feeling of love towards yourself as well.

Practice this meditation often, and attempt to go through life with a bit of that self-love glow in you all the time. For some reason, I find it particularly useful for turning bad dreams and bad drug trips around. Life itself can be seen as some kind of "trip", too, even if it moves slower; so let self love turn your life into a good trip.

A Visualisation For Power (Or, Connecting The Soul's Energy To The Body)

As I wrote the section on power, I felt intuitively drawn to the following visualisation:

I sat down with my hands placed near my crossed legs and the fingers overlapping each other, creating a half-sphere shaped hollow. In that hollow, I saw a ball of red light appear, representing my first chakra. Then, red lightening came down from above, through all my chakras and into the ball of red light. I saw this again and again; each lightening stroke seemed to help bring my soul's power more in alignment with my body. At the end of this, I felt stronger, and a lot more *solid* somehow.

Resources

Books

I wanted to read a few books to gain inspiration for this book, but in the end, I never did, and just drew from my own experience, which seemed to be enough. The only books I've really read about Wanderers are:

Indigo Children: The New Kids Have Arrived by Lee Carroll and Jan Tober - A bit of a mixed book; I mostly found inspiration in the part containing the Kryon channellings.

and parts of

The Law Of One by L/L Research and Ra

Which can be found online at www.lawofone.info.

You can search the text for information about Wanderers using the search function on the website. It explains some rather esoteric things that I hold somewhat at arm's length because I have no way of verifying their truth. However, the little practical bits of information about Wanderers fit very closely to what I already knew about indigos, making me consider this to be an authentic source of information.

Apart from books that are directly about indigos, I can also recommend:

The Power of Now by Eckhart Tolle - a deep answer to existential crises and the search for true fulfillment.

Radical Unschooling by Dayna Martin - this book presents a way of breaking down hierarchy in our parenting, and for non-parents, it is an excellent source of insight into how we can break down the hierarchy that has been inplanted in our head by the parenting that was imposed on us.

Life Before Life by Brian L. Weiss - in case you are unsure about reincarnation, this book provides solid and convincing scientific evidence. I believe that conquering your fear of death is one important step to finding inner peace, and this book can take you there, if you let it.

True Meditation by Adyashanti - An excellent guide to authentic meditation.

Psychics

Erin Pavlina - erinpavlina.com

Erin changed my life and I'll never stop singing her praises. She's pricey, though, a sad (for us - and happy for her) result of her being so successful.

Lisa MW - lisamw.com

Lisa is also great and cheaper than Erin :)

Websites

Indigo Society - indigosociety.com

A decent forum for indigos. I'd say about 50% of the people there who think they are indigo actually are. (I hope I'm not being too harsh here).

Indigo Adults Moderated - groups.yahoo.com/group/Indigo-Adults-moderated

A mailing list that I find has somewhat more civil discussion than Indigo Society.

Sunfell.com

Contains some info about indigos and crystals.

Kristen Finlayson's writings hosted at my website at sophiagubb.com/k

Kristen's advice about indigos was really helpful to me. I made a page to preserve her writings which would otherwise have disappeared.

Steve Pavlina's Blog - stevepavlina.com

Steve Pavlina writes about Personal Development and his work transformed me in many ways.

Meetup.com

If you're lucky you might find an indigo meetup near you.

You can also check **Facebook** for indigo groups, of varying usefulness.

Made in the USA
San Bernardino, CA
22 January 2018